Cascading Style Sheets in Dreamweaver CS3

About Cascading Style Sheets

Learning Objective

After completing this topic, you should be able to identify the features and functions of Cascading Style Sheets

1. Introducing CSS

When designing web sites, it is a good idea to use a consistent style so that all the individual pages have a similar appearance.

Although HTML code can be effectively used to present content, it was never intended to control the appearance of content. You can control only the basic formatting of web elements using HTML.

Cascading Style Sheets (CSS) enable you to define complex formatting styles that can be applied to individual web pages and whole web sites.

The W3C (World Wide Web Consortium) actively encourages the use of style sheets to manage the appearance of content.

By associating a style sheet with an HTML document, you can manage the document's presentation without relying on HTML extensions. Instead, you can easily define style rules in the style sheet.

CSS enables you to customize the appearance of web elements. For example, you can assign background colors, images, and borders to any HTML elements, including paragraphs.

You can use CSS to provide a complete layout or design template for your whole web site or associate mutually exclusive, alternate style sheets to a page.

There are a number of advantages to using style sheets. They enable you to

separate style and content

You can use a single style sheet to define the look for a whole site. All the presentation information is stored in a single style sheet file, so you can quickly change the appearance of the entire site. To do this, you can either edit the existing style sheet or replace it with a new one. All the web pages using the style sheet will be instantly updated.

reduce the overall amount of coding

Because you can apply a single style sheet to multiple documents, the amount of coding you need to generate is reduced. Also, because you do not need to add presentational elements and attributes to the HTML documents themselves, the HTML code becomes easier to read and manage.

exert greater control over presentation

CSS provides you with finer and more predictable control over layout and formatting. For example, you can use relative measurements in style sheets to ensure that web pages are visually appealing in multiple resolutions. You can also use them to accurately position objects and make web pages suitable for printing.

integrate multiple styles

1

Both authors and readers can apply style sheets to HTML documents. The "cascading" characteristic of CSS means that a browser applies both CSS and HTML style sheets using predefined rules to resolve any conflicts that may arise.

make content accessible

You can create specific style sheets to suit special needs. For example, a style sheet for visually impaired visitors can include style rules that increase font size. Likewise, style sheets for hearing impaired visitors can include style rules for pauses and intonation.

Although CSS is very useful, not all web browsers support all of its properties. For this reason, it is important to test a web site in a wide variety of browsers if it contains pages that use CSS. For example, you can do this by selecting **File - Preview in Browser** to test a web site as it will display in a browser.

Graphic

You select File-Preview in Browser.

Question

Why would you use CSS?

Options:

1. To create a consistent look for a web site
2. To assist in making content accessible
3. To combine style and content
4. To create sites that look identical in all browsers

Answer

Option 1: Correct. Applying a single style sheet to multiple documents ensures that each document uses the same style rules. You can change the appearance of the whole site instantly by editing or replacing the style sheet.

Option 2: Correct. Style sheets enable you to create styles to ensure that content is fully accessible. For example, you can create styles that meet the needs of visually or hearing impaired visitors.

Option 3: Incorrect. By using style sheets, you can separate style from content. This makes it easier to modify the overall appearance of content.

Option 4: Incorrect. Not all web browsers support all of the properties of CSS. When using CSS, it is important to test a site in all web browsers to ensure that it displays correctly.

Correct answer(s):

1. To create a consistent look for a web site
2. To assist in making content accessible

2. Style sheets

To control the appearance of your web pages using CSS, you need to create styles.

A style is a rule that determines how an HTML tag is formatted. For example, a style for a piece of text might define a specific font, color, and size.

Note

Regardless of the number of properties styles have, they are always identified by a single name.

A style sheet is a collection of styles that can be applied to a web page to manage the appearance of different elements.

To create styles, you need to include two main components:

a selector

The selector specifies the element that is affected by the style rule. For example, you would specify the <body> tag as the selector if you wanted to apply a style to the body of a page.

declarations

Declarations are used to define the properties of a style.

An individual declaration consists of two parts – a property and its value.

When you define styles, you enclose all the declarations for a single selector in curly braces.

In an example, a style has been defined using two declarations. The properties are font-family and background-color, and their values, respectively, are "Times" and "yellow."

Code

```
body {
  font-family: Times;
  background-color: yellow;
}
```

There are three ways that you can apply styles to a web page:

using an external style sheet

External style sheets are separate documents that contain only CSS code. A single external style sheet can be linked to multiple web pages to create consistent formatting.

using an internal style sheet

Internal style sheets contain styles that are stored in the <head> section of the HTML code for the web page itself. These styles will apply only to the web page that they are stored in.

using inline styles

You can apply a style to a single tag in a web page by placing the style within the tag that you want to format.

The cascading characteristic of CSS refers to the order in which styles are applied to a document. This order is necessary to prevent conflict when multiple style rules affect the same tag. The order of precedence is:

- inline style

- embedded style

- external style

Suppose an external style sheet, an internal style sheet, and various inline styles are used in a single web page.

If a property in the embedded style sheet conflicts with the same property in the external style rule, the value of the property in the embedded style sheet is used.

Likewise, if an inline style rule property conflicts with an embedded style rule property, the value of the inline style rule property is used.

Question

There are three main ways that you can apply styles.

Match each type of style sheet with the way that its styles are applied.

Options:

    A.   External style sheet

B. Internal style sheet

C. Inline style rule

Targets:

1. Styles are stored in a document containing only CSS code
2. Styles are stored in the <head> section of a web page's HTML code
3. Styles are placed within individual tags in a single web page

Answer

External style sheets are separate documents that contain only CSS code. You can link external style sheets to whole web sites or single pages.

Internal style sheets contain styles that are stored in the <head> section of the HTML code for a web page itself. These styles will apply only to the web page that they are stored in.

Inline styles are applied to a single tag in a web page. The style is placed within the tag that you want to format.

Correct answer(s):

Target 1 = Option A

Target 2 = Option B

Target 3 = Option C

The cascading order of style sheets determines not only which style rule is used, but also which style properties within a specific style sheet are inherited by elements within the document.

There are three types of style rules you can use in a style sheet:

tag style rules

A tag style rule specifies a set of properties for a standard HTML tag, such as <body>.

class style rules

A class style rule specifies a custom style that you can apply as a class attribute to any tag.

advanced style rules

An advanced style rule specifies a set of properties for a combination of tags.

The rules of inheritance need to be applied when more than one style rule applies to content in a document.

Suppose you have applied a specific style to a word in a paragraph, but you have also defined a style for all paragraph tags.

The rules of inheritance determine which properties of the tag style rule and which properties of the class style rule need to be applied to the word.

With regard to the inheritance of style rule properties,

- class style rule properties take precedence over tag style rule properties

- nested tag style rule properties take precedence over parent tag style rule properties

Some style rule properties cannot be inherited. You can consult the CSS Reference included with Dreamweaver CS3 to check whether a property is inheritable. You access this by selecting **Help - Reference**.

Only in rare circumstances will you need to investigate whether a property is inheritable. The CSS specification was carefully considered and inheritance usually works exactly as expected.

Suppose you have created a style sheet containing three style rules:

Code

```
p {
  font-family: Arial;
  font-weight: normal;
  color: green;
}
em {
  font-weight: bold;
  color: blue;
}
.codeRed {
  font-style: italic;
```

```
  color: red;
}
```

- a tag style for the \<p\> tag

- a tag style for the \<em\> tag

- a class style, .codeRed

You apply the style sheet to a web page containing basic HTML code.

Due to inheritance, the word "walk" is styled in

Code

```
<html>
<head>
<style type="text/css">
p {
  font-family: Arial;
  font-weight: normal;
  color: green;
}
em {
  font-weight: bold;
  color: blue;
}
.codeRed {
  font-style: italic;
  color: red;
}
</style>
</head>
<body>
<p>In case of emergency, <em class="codeRed">walk</em> to the nearest exit.</p>
</body>
</html>
```

Arial

The font-family property of the \<p\> tag style rule has a value of "Arial," which causes the word "walk" to appear in the Arial font.

bold

Because the \<em\> tag is nested in the \<p\> tag, it inherits the \<p\> tag's style rule properties. If there is no conflict, the \<p\> tag's style rule properties are added to the \<em\> tag's style rule properties. In this case, because there is a conflict, the color and font-weight properties are overridden and the font-family property is inherited. The value of the font-weight property is "bold" because there is no font-weight property in the .codeRed class style rule that overrides it.

red

The .codeRed class tag is nested inside the <em> tag. This means the .codeRed class tag inherits the <em> tag's style rule properties – color, font-weight, and font-family. However, the value of the .codeRed color property conflicts with that of the inherited color property. Because class style rule properties take precedence over tag style rule properties, the red value takes precedence over the inherited blue value.

italic

The .codeRed class style rule contains a property of its own – the font-style property, whose value is "italic." The value of this property cannot be overridden and is added directly to the final styling.

Summary

Cascading Style Sheets (CSS) enable you to define formatting styles that can be applied to individual web pages and whole web sites. They enable you to customize the appearance of web elements.

A style is a rule that determines how an HTML tag is formatted, and a style sheet is a collection of these styles. You can use an external style sheet, an internal style sheet, or an inline style rule. The cascading characteristic of CSS refers to the order in which style rules are applied.

The cascading characteristic of style sheets also determines which style rule properties are overridden and which are inherited.

CSS in Dreamweaver CS3

Learning Objectives

After completing this topic, you should be able to

- *set CSS Styles preferences*
- *recognize the features of the CSS Styles panel*

1. Setting CSS Styles preferences

Dreamweaver CS3 includes many features that enable you to use Cascading Style Sheets (CSS) to create styles and layouts for your web pages.

CSS enables you to define formatting rules that control the appearance of elements on one or more web pages.

Before using CSS, it is helpful to set various preferences. CSS style preferences manage the way that Dreamweaver creates CSS code.

To begin setting the CSS style preferences, you select **Edit - Preferences**.

Note

*If you are using a Macintosh computer, you select **Dreamweaver - Preferences**.*

The Preferences dialog box opens.

Graphic

The Preferences dialog box contains a Category list box that enables you to choose the category of Dreamweaver preferences that you want to configure. By default, the General category is selected.

To access options for CSS styles, you select **CSS Styles** from the Category list.

The CSS Styles section of the Preferences dialog box enables you to configure the style options that you want to apply. There are three main sections.

When creating CSS rules

The "When creating CSS rules" section enables you to specify which CSS style properties Dreamweaver must write in shorthand. You can choose to use shorthand for the font, background, margin and padding, border and border width, and list style when creating CSS rules.

The "When creating CSS rules" section has five checkboxes – Font, Background, Margin and padding, Border and border width, and List-Style.

When editing CSS rules

The "When editing CSS rules" section enables you to choose to use shorthand either if the original style used shorthand, or in accordance with the preferences that you have set for creating CSS styles. You can also specify whether you want a CSS style to open automatically when you modify it.

The "When editing CSS rules" section has two radio buttons – If original used shorthand and According to settings above – and an Open CSS files when modified checkbox.

When double-clicking in CSS panel

The "When double-clicking in CSS panel" section enables you to specify which tool you want to use to edit CSS styles. You can use the CSS dialog box, the Properties pane, or Code view.

The "When double-clicking in CSS panel" section has three radio buttons – Edit using CSS dialog, Edit using Properties pane, and Edit using code view.

In this instance, you want to use shorthand when creating CSS styles for fonts and backgrounds only, so you select the **Font** and **Background** checkboxes.

You also specify that shorthand should be used only if the original style was created using shorthand by selecting the **If original used shorthand** radio button.

You then choose to edit the CSS styles using the CSS dialog box by selecting the **Edit using CSS dialog** radio button, and click **OK** to accept the new settings.

The CSS style preferences are now set and you can begin to create and edit styles.

SkillCheck

You want to begin creating CSS styles so that you can manage the appearance of elements on a web page. You decide to use shorthand when creating CSS styles for fonts and to use shorthand when editing styles only if styles were originally created using it. To edit CSS styles, you want to use the Properties pane.

Set the appropriate CSS style preferences.

Task:

1. Access the dialog box that enables you to set preferences.

2. Access preferences for CSS styles.

3. Specify and accept the CSS style settings.

Answer

To complete the task

*Step 1: Select **Edit - Preferences***

*Step 2: Select **CSS Styles** from the Category list*

*Step 3: Select the **Font** checkbox, the **If original used shorthand** radio button, and the **Edit using Properties pane** radio button, and then click **OK***

2. The CSS Styles panel

The CSS Styles panel enables you to manage CSS styles.

If it's not open or expanded, you can access this panel by selecting **Window - CSS Styles**.

Alternatively, you can click **CSS Styles** in the panels group to expand the panel.

You can choose one of two modes in which to view the CSS panel.

You can either use All mode to access information about all the CSS styles that apply to the page, or you can use Current mode to access information about the style that applies to the element that is currently selected in the page.

Graphic

The CSS Styles panel contains two buttons that enable you to switch views – All and Current.

If you choose to view the CSS panel in All mode, it is divided into two main panes:

All Rules

The All Rules pane lists all the CSS styles that have been defined for the current page. Any styles that have been defined in the style sheets that are attached to the document are also included.

Properties

The Properties pane enables you to edit the properties of the CSS styles that are listed in the All Rules pane.

When you select a style in the All Rules pane, all of the properties for that style rule are shown in the Properties pane.

Graphic

The #Layer1 style is selected in the All Rules pane and the properties for this rule are listed in the Properties pane. There are currently six properties that have been set – height, left, position, top, width, and z-index.

9

You want to modify the style rule for .style1. To begin, you select this style in the All Rules pane and the associated properties are listed in the Properties pane.

Graphic

.style1 is selected in the All Rules pane. There are three properties that have been set – color, font-family, and font-weight.

Note

By default, only the properties that have been previously set are shown in the Properties pane.

Try It

You want to change the font-family property for the CSS style rule.

To complete the task

1. Select **font-family** in the Property pane
2. Select **Verdana, Arial, Helvetica**, click the down-pointing arrow that appears, and select **Arial, Helvetica, sans-serif**

The CSS style rule is modified.

The changes that you make to CSS styles are applied immediately after you have edited them and you can view the changes on the page. In this example, the font used for the title has changed.

You can change the view of the CSS Styles panel by clicking the **Current** button.

Current mode splits the CSS Styles panel into three sections.

Summary for Selection

The Summary for Selection section shows the CSS properties for the element that is currently selected on the page.

Rules

The Rules section indicates the location of the property that is selected in the Properties pane.

Properties

The Properties section enables you to edit the CSS properties for the element that is currently selected.

In this example, you have selected the heading in the web page. The style named .style1 applies to this selection, so the CSS properties defined for this style are shown in the Summary for Selection pane.

Graphic

The three properties that have been set are color, font-family, and font-weight.

The Rules pane indicates that the these properties are located in the <p> tag.

The Properties pane enables you to edit the three properties that have already been defined for the style. You can also add CSS properties to the style by selecting one of the properties that is currently undefined.

In both All mode and Current mode, you can choose between three views for the CSS Styles panel using the buttons on the left corner of the panel.

Show category view

The **Show category view** button shows the CSS styles by category. This view splits the CSS properties into eight categories – font, background, block, border, box, list, positioning, and extensions.

The properties for each category are shown in a list that you can expand or collapse. Properties that have been set are shown at the top of the list.

Show list view

The **Show list view** button shows the CSS styles in list view. This view enables you to view all the CSS styles in alphabetical order. Properties that have been set are shown at the top of the list.

Show only set

The **Show only set** properties button shows only the properties that have been set. This view is the default view.

You can resize any of the panes in the CSS Styles panel by dragging the borders between the panes.

Graphic

The Properties pane is resized.

The CSS Styles panel contains four buttons that enable you to manage the CSS styles that are used for a page.

Attach Style Sheet

The **Attach Style Sheet** button enables you to choose an external style sheet to link to or import into your current page.

New CSS Rule

The **New CSS Rule** button enables you to specify the type of style that you want to create. For example, you can create a class style or define a CSS selector.

Edit Style

The **Edit Style** button enables you to modify the styles that are used in the current document or that are contained in an external style sheet.

Delete CSS Rule

The **Delete CSS Rule** button enables you to remove rules or properties from the CSS Styles panel. You can also remove formatting from elements and detach CSS style sheets that have been attached to the page.

Question

The CSS Styles panel enables you to manage the CSS styles that apply to the current page.

What can you do using the CSS Styles panel?

Options:

1. Modify CSS style rules that have already been created
2. Access all properties that apply to a selected element
3. Attach an external style sheet to the current web page
4. Create new CSS style sheets to attach to other web pages
5. Attach a custom style sheet template to a web page

Answer

Option 1: Correct. You can use the Properties pane in the CSS panel to edit any CSS styles that have already been defined.

Option 2: Correct. When you select an element on a web page, any CSS style properties that apply to it are listed in the CSS panel.

Option 3: Correct. The **Attach Style Sheet** button on the CSS panel enables you to choose an external style sheet to link to or import into your current page.

Option 4: Incorrect. You cannot create new CSS style sheets using the CSS Styles panel. However, you can use the CSS Styles panel to create new CSS styles and to attach external style sheets to a web page.

Option 5: Incorrect. You cannot use the CSS Styles panel to attach a custom style sheet template to a web page. You can use the CSS Styles panel only to attach an external style sheet to a web page or to define CSS styles.

Correct answer(s):

1. Modify CSS style rules that have already been created
2. Access all properties that apply to a selected element
3. Attach an external style sheet to the current web page

Summary

Dreamweaver CS3 enables you to set Cascading Style Sheet (CSS) style preferences so that you can manage the way that CSS styles are created. You can modify the way that CSS styles are created and edited, and choose which tool to use to edit styles.

The CSS Styles panel enables you to manage CSS styles for the current page. You can access this panel in either All mode or Current mode.

Creating Style Sheets and Rules in Dreamweaver CS3

Learning Objectives

After completing this topic, you should be able to

- *create a style sheet*
- *create a style rule*

1. Creating style sheets

Style sheets enable you to manage the appearance of elements on web pages.

A Cascading Style Sheet (CSS) is a text file, saved with the .css extension, that contains a collection of style rules.

You can use Dreamweaver CS3 to easily create style sheets and define style rules.

There are three main types of style rules that you can add to a style sheet:

- rules that specify properties for a standard HTML tag

- rules that create custom styles that you can apply as a class attribute to any tag

- rules that specify properties for a combination of tags

To begin creating a style sheet, you select **File - New**.

The New Document dialog box opens.

Graphic

The New Document dialog box enables you to specify the type of document you want to create, its page type, and the layout of the new document.

Try It

You want to create a blank CSS document.

To complete the task

1. Select **CSS** in the Page Type list box and click **Create**

A new CSS file is created.

When you create a blank CSS file, the style sheet that is created contains no styles.

You can add style rules immediately by typing the relevant CSS code.

Note

CSS files can be created only in Code view. The Design view is disabled by default.

You can also use the CSS Styles panel to add and manage the style rules that you want to include in the new style sheet.

Graphic

The CSS Styles panel lists any style rules that have been defined, and shows their properties.

It includes seven buttons – Show category view, Show list view, Show only set properties, Attach Style Sheet, New CSS Rule, Edit Style, and Delete Style.

You want to use the CSS Styles panel to add a style rule to the style sheet that you have just created.

To begin, you click the **New CSS Rule** button.

The New CSS Rule dialog box opens.

Graphic

The New CSS Rule dialog box has three main sections – Selector Type, Name, and Define in.

In the Selector Type section of the New CSS Rule dialog box, there are three radio buttons that enable you to define the type of style rule that you want to create.

Class (can apply to any tag)

The **Class (can apply to any tag)** option enables you to create a class style rule. You can either type a name for the style in the Name text box or select one from the drop-down list. A class name should begin with a period.

Tag (redefines the look of a specific tag)

The **Tag (redefines the look of a specific tag)** option enables you to create a tag style rule. You can either type the name of the tag in the Tag text box or select one from the drop-down list.

Advanced (IDs, pseudo-class selectors)

The **Advanced (IDs, pseudo-class selectors)** option enables you to create an advanced style rule. You can either type the name of the selector tag in the Selector text box or select one from the drop-down list.

The Define in section enables you to specify the style sheet that you want the style rule to be attached to. There are two options.

(New Style Sheet File)

You can use the (New Style Sheet File) drop-down list to add the style rule to an existing external style sheet or a new external style sheet.

If there are no existing external style sheets attached to the current document, the **(New Style Sheet File)** option is automatically selected in the drop-down list.

This document only

You can use the **This document only** option to create an embedded rule.

In this instance, you want to define a style rule for the heading tag, h1.

To begin, you select the **Tag (redefines the look of a specific tag)** radio button in the Selector Type section.

The Name drop-down list box is automatically replaced by a Tag drop-down list box. You choose the **h1** option from the Tag drop-down list.

Graphic

The Tag drop-down menu lists all the tags that you can add style rules to for the current page.

In the Define in section, the option to add the rule to the current document is selected by default.

To accept the settings you've chosen, you click **OK**.

The CSS Rule definition for h1 dialog box opens. There are eight categories in the Category list box, each containing various style options that you can use to define style rules.

Graphic

The CSS Rule definition for h1 dialog box contains a Category list box and a pane that displays options in the currently selected category.

Type

The Type category enables you to define basic font and type properties. For example, you can manage font, size, style, weight, case, and color.

Background

The Background category enables you to define background properties. You can specify a background color or image. If you define a background image, you can specify whether it must be repeated and whether it must scroll along with the content. You can also specify its initial position within the element.

Block

The Block category enables you to define spacing and alignment properties for tags and attributes. For example, you can manage word spacing, letter spacing, vertical alignment, and text indentation. Many browsers do not support block-level rules.

Box

The Box category enables you to define properties for tags and attributes that control the placement of elements on a page. For example, you can manage the width, height, padding, and margins of elements.

Border

The Border category enables you to define properties for the borders around elements. For example, you can manage the width, color, and style of borders. You must specify a style, width, and color for each side of a border that you want to appear on a page. If you do not want a border to appear on a particular side, you must explicitly set its width to zero.

List

The List category enables you to define settings such as bullet size, type, and position for list tags. List properties should be used only with list and list item elements.

Positioning

The Positioning category enables you to define layer positioning attributes so that you can specify the exact placement of an element within a page.

Extensions

The Extensions category enables you to define properties for page breaks and visual effects.

You can define page breaks either before or after an element.

You can also define a Cursor property that changes the pointer image when the pointer is positioned over an element, and a Filter property that applies a special effect to an element.

To define the style rule for the h1 tag, you accept the default selection of the Type category.

Graphic

The CSS Rule definition for h1 dialog box shows the options for the Type category. For example, you can set font size, style, and weight.

Try It

You now want to define a style rule to control the font used.

To complete the task

1. Select **Arial, Helvetica, sans-serif** from the Font drop-down list and click **OK**

The style rule is created.

The code is added to the style sheet.

Graphic

The following code is added:

```
h1 {
font-family: Arial, Helvetica, sans-serif;
}
```

The style rule is also listed in the All Rules pane on the CSS Styles panel.

Graphic

The style rule, h1, is listed in the All Rules pane.

After creating a style sheet, you can save it by selecting **File - Save**.

In the Save As dialog box, you specify a location and name for the style sheet and then click **Save**.

The style sheet is automatically saved with the .css extension.

Question

You have created a new style sheet and now want to add a style rule to it.

How do you do this?

Options:

1. Choose to add a new rule, specify the selector type and where the rule will be defined, and then configure the properties for the rule
2. Choose to add a new rule, specify the HTML type and where the rule will be defined, and then configure the properties for the rule
3. Add a new style rule, specify the tag type and which external style sheet the rule will be defined in, and then set the style properties

Answer

Option 1: Correct. To create a new style rule, you need to specify whether the rule will be a class, tag, or advanced style rule. You also need to specify whether it will be defined in the current document or in a new style sheet. You can then define the style properties.

Option 2: Incorrect. You need to specify the selector type when creating a new style rule. You can create class, tag, or advanced style rules.

Option 3: Incorrect. When you create a new style rule, you can define it in an external style sheet or in the current document.

Correct answer(s):

1. Choose to add a new rule, specify the selector type and where the rule will be defined, and then configure the properties for the rule

SkillCheck

You want to use a style sheet to manage the appearance of your web page.

Use the New Document dialog box to create a new CSS style sheet.

Task:

1. Access the dialog box that enables you to create a new document.
2. Select the type of file that you want to create and create it.

Answer

To complete the task

*Step 1: Select **File - New***

2. Applying styles to web pages

You can attach an existing style sheet to a web page to apply the style rules to the contents of the page.

To begin, you need to open the page to which you want to attach the style sheet.

You then select **Text - CSS Styles - Attach Style Sheet**.

Alternatively, you can click the **Attach Style Sheet** button on the CSS Styles panel.

The Attach External Style Sheet dialog box opens, enabling you to specify the external style sheet that you want to attach to the document.

There are four main settings.

File/URL drop-down list

The File/URL drop-down list enables you to specify the location of the external style sheet. You can type a path, select one from the drop-down list, or use the associated **Browse** button to browse to the location of the style sheet.

Add as section

The Add as section enables you to choose whether you want to link or import the external style sheet.

The **Link** option creates a link between the document and the external style sheet. It is supported by Microsoft Internet Explorer and Mozilla Firefox.

The **Import** option is most often used to nest one external style sheet within another. You can use it to import an external style sheet into a document. However, not all browsers support this function.

Media drop-down list

The Media drop-down list enables you to specify the media type that the style sheet is designed for.

sample style sheets link

The **sample style sheets** link enables you to access various external style sheets that you can either modify or apply directly to your web pages.

In the Attach External Style Sheet dialog box, you need to specify the external style sheet you want to attach, so you click the **Browse** button.

The Select Style Sheet File dialog box opens, and you locate the style sheet you want to attach and click **OK**.

Graphic

The Select Style Sheet File dialog box lists the files that you can add. The file Northglenn.css is selected.

The name of the style sheet you selected – Northglenn.css – displays in the File/URL text box.

By default, the **Link** option in the Add as section is selected. You keep this setting and continue by selecting **all** from the Media drop-down list.

Graphic

There are nine options in the Media drop-down list – all, aural, braille, handheld, print, projection, screen, tty, and tv.

You then click **OK** to close the Attach External Style Sheet dialog box.

The external style sheet is attached to the page and the styles it defines are applied to the content.

As an alternative to using an existing style sheet to format a page, you can create new style sheets and style rules directly within an HTML document.

When you create a style rule while editing a particular document, Dreamweaver CS3 automatically enables you to attach the rule either to the current style sheet for the document or to a new style sheet.

Try It

You want to create a new style rule to manage the appearance of the body tag of the new page that you have opened.

To complete the task

1. Select **Text - CSS Styles - New**

The New CSS Rule dialog box opens.

You want to create a tag style rule in a new style sheet. So you select the **Tag (redefines the look of a specific tag)** radio button and the **(New Style Sheet File)** radio button, and select the portion of the page the rule will apply to – body – in the Tag drop-down list box.

Graphic

The New CSS Rule dialog box contains a Selector Type section with three radio buttons – Class (can apply to any tag), Tag (redefines the look of a specific tag), and Advanced (IDs, pseudo-class selectors). It includes a Selector drop-down list box, and a Define in section with a (New Style Sheet File) radio button and a "This document only" radio button. Once the Tag (redefines the look of a specific tag) radio button is selected, the Selector drop-down list box is replaced by a Tag drop-down list box.

You then click **OK**.

When you close the New CSS Rule dialog box, the Save Style Sheet File As dialog box opens automatically, enabling you to name the external style sheet that you are creating.

You type the name – yogastyles in this case – in the File name text box and then click **Save**.

The Save Style Sheet File As dialog box closes and the CSS Rule definition for body dialog box opens.

Graphic

The CSS Rule definition for body dialog box contains a Category list box in which Type is selected by default. With this category selected, it displays Font, Size, Weight, Style, Variant, and Line height, and Case drop-down lists, a Color picker, and a Decoration section with five checkboxes – underline, overline, line-through, blink, and none.

You define the style rule using the options in the CSS Rule definition for .typeface dialog box and click **OK**.

Graphic

In this example, you select Verdana, Arial, Helvetica, sans-serif from the Font drop-down list, normal from the Weight drop-down list, normal from the Style drop-down list, and #666666 from the Color panel.

Dreamweaver CS3 automatically attaches the new style sheet to the HTML document and lists the style rule in the CSS Styles panel.

Graphic

The style sheet yogastyles.css and the style rule named "body" are listed in the All Rules pane of the CSS Styles panel.

Question

You do not want to use an existing style sheet to format a page.

How do you create a style rule in a new style sheet from directly within an HTML document?

Options:

1. Open a web page, add a new CSS style rule, choose to add the rule to a new style sheet, and then name and save the new style sheet
2. Add a new CSS style rule to the current web page, choose to add the rule to the existing style sheet, and then name and save the new style sheet
3. Open a style sheet, save the style rule in this style sheet, and then save the style sheet with a new name within the web page

Answer

Option 1: Correct. When you create a new CSS style rule, you have the option to create it in a new style sheet. You then need to name and save the new style sheet before defining the rule.

Option 2: Incorrect. To create a new style sheet, you need to choose to add the style rule to a new style sheet.

Option 3: Incorrect. To create a style rule in a new style sheet, you cannot use an existing style sheet.

Correct answer(s):

1. Open a web page, add a new CSS style rule, choose to add the rule to a new style sheet, and then name and save the new style sheet

SkillCheck

You want to use an external style sheet to manage the appearance of the current web page.

Use the CSS Styles panel to attach the style sheet named "newstyles.css" to the current page.

Task:

1. Access options for attaching a style sheet.
2. Access the dialog box that enables you to select a file.
3. Choose the file that you want to attach.
4. Attach the style sheet to the web page.

Answer

To complete the task

*Step 1: Click the **Attach Style Sheet** button on the CSS Styles panel*

*Step 2: Click the **Browse** button*

*Step 3: Select **newstyles** and click **OK***

*Step 4: Click **OK***

3. Adding embedded and inline styles

You can apply specific styles to individual pages using embedded style rules.

Embedded styles are not stored in an external CSS file, but are rather located in the HTML code of a specific web page. They apply only to the web page that they are located in.

You want to add an embedded style to one of the individual web pages in the Northglenn web site.

To begin, you ensure that the relevant page – in this instance aboutus.html – is open.

You want to apply a style to the link tags on the page, so you position the cursor in one of the links.

Then you click the **New CSS Rule** button in the CSS Styles panel.

The New CSS Rule dialog box opens, with the **Tag (redefines the look of a specific tag)** radio button selected by default.

The **a** option is also automatically selected in the Tag drop-down list box.

To define an embedded tag style rule for the tag, you ensure that the **This document only** option is selected in the Define in section and then click **OK**.

You now need to define the properties for the tag using the "CSS Rule definition for a" dialog box.

To begin, you want to change the color of the hyperlinks on the page. So you change the Color property.

Try It

You also want to modify the font.

To complete the task

1. Select **Courier New, Courier, monospace** from the Font drop-down list and click **OK**

The style rule for hyperlink tags is set.

The style rule is applied to all the link tags on the page.

The embedded style rule is also added within a style element in the <head> tag of the HTML code.

Graphic

The following code is added to the HTML code:

```
a {
font-family; "Courier New", Courier, monospace;
color: #990033;
}
```

SkillCheck

You want to apply a specific style to the heading tags, h1, of an individual page.

Add an embedded style to the current page to define the appearance of its headings.

Task:

1. Add a new CSS style rule.
2. Specify the type of tag that you want to create the rule for.
3. Specify that the rule should be embedded in the current document.

Answer

To complete the task

*Step 1: Click the **New CSS Rule** button on the CSS Styles panel*

*Step 2: Select **h1** from the Tag drop-down list*

*Step 3: Select **This document only** and click **OK***

You can apply styles to specific elements on a web page using inline styles.

An inline style rule is a style rule that is applied directly to content. This style rule is defined within the element itself.

Inline style rules override any style rules that have been specified in an embedded or external style sheet.

You want to apply a style to the heading on the current web page, but do not want it to be applied to any of the other headings.

Note

If you apply this formatting using the Property inspector, the text format will be added to the page as an embedded style rule.

You decide to use an inline style rule to change the formatting of the heading.

To begin, you click the **Code** button to access the page's HTML code.

Graphic

The HTML code for the relevant tag is

<p align="center">Welcome</p>

To create an inline style rule, you need to add the style attribute and the required properties in the relevant tag.

You click in the tag and then type the code that will define the style.

Graphic

THe HTML code is now

<p align="center" style ="color: red; margin-left: 17px;">Welcome</p>

You click the **Design** button. The formatting of the first heading has now changed to reflect the style rule that you have added.

Graphic

The color of the title has changed.

Question

You want to define an inline style rule so that the style is applied only to an individual element on your page.

How do you do this?

Options:

1. Access the HTML code for the web page, locate the tag that you want the style to apply to, and then type the code within the style attribute for this tag
2. Access the CSS code for the web page, locate the attribute that you want the style to apply to, and then type the code within the CSS attribute for this tag

23

3. View the web page in code view, locate the tag that you want the style to apply to, and then type the code within the body attribute for this tag

Answer

Option 1: Correct. To apply an inline style rule, you need to type the relevant code in the style attribute for the tag that you want to format.

Option 2: Incorrect. To create an inline style rule, you need to add to the HTML code by typing within the style attribute for the tag that you want to format.

Option 3: Incorrect. An inline style rule must be defined within the style attribute of the tag you want to format.

Correct answer(s):

1. Access the HTML code for the web page, locate the tag that you want the style to apply to, and then type the code within the style attribute for this tag

Summary

You can create Cascading Style Sheets (CSS) style sheets in Dreamweaver CS3 to manage the appearance of web pages. To create an external style sheet, you create a new CSS file and then add and define style rules.

External style sheets can be attached to individual pages or whole web sites. You can also create new style sheets and style rules from directly within an HTML document if you do not want to use an external style sheet.

Embedded and inline styles can be used to format web pages. Embedded styles are located in the HTML code of a specific web page. They apply only to the web pages that they are located in. An inline style rule is a style rule that is applied directly to content. This style rule is defined within the HTML code for the element itself.

Modifying Style Sheets and Rules in Dreamweaver CS3

Learning Objectives

After completing this topic, you should be able to

- *edit a style rule*
- *identify the new CSS management features*
- *edit a style sheet*

1. New CSS management features

Dreamweaver CS3 enables you to use Cascading Style Sheets (CSS) to manage the appearance of your web pages. It also provides features that make it easy for you to manage the CSS style rules and style sheets that you create.

Using the new CSS management features, you can now easily move CSS rules to different locations. For example, you can move rules from one document to another, from the head of a document to an external style sheet, or between external CSS files.

Note

Embedded style rules apply only to the document in which they are embedded, so if you want to use an embedded style rule in a document other than the one that it was created in, you need to move it to an external style sheet and then attach this style sheet to the document.

Suppose you want to move a CSS style rule that you have created to a different style sheet.

To begin, you need to expand the CSS panel group by selecting **Window - CSS Styles**.

Keyboard Sequence

*The keyboard alternative is **Shift+F11**.*

When you open the CSS Styles panel in All mode, the All Rules pane of the panel lists all the style sheets that are attached to your current document.

Graphic

The CSS Styles panel has two main panes – All Rules and Properties.

Each style sheet and the style rules that it contains are listed in the All Rules pane.

The properties of the style rule that is selected in the All Rules pane are listed in the Properties pane.

In this instance, there is an embedded style sheet, indicated by a <style> tag, and an external style sheet, Northglenn.css.

You can access the style rules that are contained in each style sheet by expanding the style sheet node in the All Rules pane on the CSS Styles panel.

Graphic

The <style> style sheet is expanded in the All Rules pane.

You want to move a style rule from the embedded rule named .style8 to a different style sheet.

To do this, you begin by right-clicking the style rule in the All Rules pane.

Next you select **Move CSS Rules** from the menu that displays.

The Move to External Style Sheet dialog box opens, enabling you to specify the style sheet to which you want to move the style rule.

Graphic

The Move to External Style Sheet dialog box contains a Style sheet radio button with a corresponding drop-down list box and a Browse button, and a "A new style sheet" radio button. The Style sheet radio button is selected by default.

The **Style sheet** option enables you to move a style rule to an existing style sheet. You can select the style sheet from the drop-down list or locate the file by browsing for it.

The **A new style sheet** option enables you to create a new style sheet to move the style rule to.

Try It

You want to move the selected style rule to an existing style sheet called "newstyles."

To complete the task

1. Click the **Browse** button
2. Select **newstyles** and click **OK**
   The Select Style Sheet File dialog box opens, enabling you to choose a CSS file.
3. Click **OK**

The style rule is moved to the specified style sheet.

After you move a style rule, the style sheet to which you've moved the style rule is listed in the All Rules pane on the CSS Styles panel.

Graphic

The style rule named .style8 is now listed in the All Rules pane in the newstyles.css style sheet.

Dreamweaver's new CSS management features enable you to move style rules by dragging them from one location to another in the CSS Styles panel.

You can drag style rules to modify their order within a style sheet, or to move a style rule to another style sheet or the document head.

Say you want to move the style rule named #image from its current location to the external style sheet named newstyles.css.

To do this, you select the style rule and then drag it to the newstyles file in the All Rules pane on the CSS Styles panel.

Graphic

The style rule is dragged from its current location to the newstyles style sheet.

The style rule is now contained in the external style sheet.

Graphic

The style rule, #image, is now listed in the newstyles.css style sheet on the CSS Styles panel.

If you want to move more than one style rule to a new location, you can select multiple files in the CSS Styles panel and then drag them to the new location.

To select multiple files, you press **Ctrl** and then click each file that you want to move.

Note

*On a Macintosh you press **Command** before selecting each file that you want to move.*

Once you have selected the files, you can drag them to a new location.

The style rules are moved to the external style sheet, newstyles.css.

Using inline styles is not a recommended best practice. Dreamweaver CS3 now enables you to make your CSS cleaner and more organized by easily converting inline styles to CSS rules.

You can convert inline styles to CSS styles that are contained in the head of the document or in an external style sheet.

Try It

To convert an inline style rule, you first need to access the document's code.

To complete the task

1. Click the **Show Code view** button

The code is shown.

To begin, you need to select the entire <style> tag that contains the inline style rule that you want to convert.

Graphic

The following tag is selected:

<p style="color: #000000;">

Next you right-click the tag and select **CSS Styles - Convert Inline CSS to Rule**.

Note

*Alternatively, you select the tag, and select **Text - CSS Styles - Convert Inline CSS to Rule**.*

The Convert Inline CSS dialog box opens. You can specify the type of style rule to which you want to convert the inline style and enter a name for the new rule using the Convert to drop-down list and text box.

Graphic

The Convert Inline CSS dialog box contains a Convert to drop-down list box and a "Create rule in" section. The Create rule in section has a Style sheet radio button with a corresponding drop-down list box and a Browse button, and a "The head of this document" radio button.

You can specify whether you want the style rule to be contained in a style sheet or in the head of the document using options in the "Create rule in" section.

In this instance, you name the style rule .style15.

You want the converted style rule to be contained in the external style sheet newstyles.css, so you ensure that the **Style sheet** radio button is selected and that this style sheet is specified.

You then click **OK** to convert the inline style rule.

The inline style rule is converted to a CSS style.

Question

Dreamweaver CS3 provides new CSS management features.

What can you do using these features?

Options:

1. Move CSS style rules from an embedded style sheet to an external style sheet
2. Convert inline style rules to CSS styles that are contained in the head of a document
3. Convert style rules that are contained in an external style sheet to inline style rules
4. Convert style rules that are contained in an embedded style sheet to inline style rules

Answer

Option 1: Correct. You can move style rules from one document to another, from the head of a document to an external style sheet or between external CSS files.

Option 2: Correct. Using inline styles is not a recommended best practice. You can convert inline styles to CSS styles that are contained in the head of the document or in an external style sheet.

Option 3: Incorrect. Using inline styles is not a recommended best practice. You can convert inline style rules to external style rules.

Option 4: Incorrect. Using inline styles is not a recommended best practice. You can convert inline style rules to embedded style rules.

Correct answer(s):

1. Move CSS style rules from an embedded style sheet to an external style sheet
2. Convert inline style rules to CSS styles that are contained in the head of a document

2. Editing style rules

You can edit CSS style rules after they have been created to easily modify the appearance of web pages and web sites.

You want to update the appearance of the Northglenn Fitness Club web site by modifying some of the styles that you have applied to it.

Try It

You decide to modify the style rule named .style1 in the embedded style sheet.

To complete the task

1. Select **.style1** in the CSS Styles panel
2. Click the **Edit Style** button

The CSS Rule definition dialog box opens.

The Type category is selected by default in the Category list. Options in this category enable you to change things like the font family, the font size, and whether the text is plain or bold.

The current font is set to the Verdana, Arial, Helvetica, sans-serif family, and you decide to leave it that way.

Graphic

The CSS Rule definition for .style1 dialog box contains a Category list box in which Type is selected by default. With this category selected, it displays Font, Size, Weight, Style, Variant, Line height, and Case drop-down lists, a color picker, and a Decoration section with five checkboxes – underline, overline, line-through, blink, and none.

To change the font weight from bold to normal, you select **normal** from the Weight drop-down list.

You also want to modify the font color, so you click the color picker and select a new color.

To apply the changes to the style rule, you click **OK**.

The changes that you made are automatically applied to the document.

You can edit style rules directly using the Properties pane in the CSS Styles panel.

Say you want to edit the style rule named .style13. You begin by selecting this style in the All Rules pane.

The style's properties are then listed in the Properties pane.

Graphic

There are two defined properties – color and font-weight.

Try It

You now want to modify the font weight – which is currently set to bold – for the selected style.

To complete the task

1. Select **font-weight** in the Properties pane

2. Click the down-pointing arrow that displays in the value field for the property and select **normal** from the drop-down list

The style rule is modified.

In addition to editing the properties of a style rule, you can change the name of a style.

You want to change the name of the .style1 style rule to "heading."

To begin, you right-click the style rule in the All Rules pane and select **Rename Class** from the menu that displays.

The Rename Class dialog box opens, enabling you to choose the style rule that you want to rename and to specify the new name.

The style rule that you selected is shown in the Rename class drop-down list by default.

Graphic

The Rename Class dialog box has a Rename class drop-down list box and a New name text box.

You enter the modified name in the New name text box and click **OK**.

The name of the style rule is changed. The new name is now shown in the All Rules section of the CSS Styles panel.

Question

You can edit style rules to modify the appearance of web pages.

What changes can you make to style rules in Dreamweaver CS3?

Options:

1. Change the properties of style rules
2. Modify the names of style rules
3. Change the file extensions of style rules
4. Edit the categories of style rule properties

Answer

Option 1: Correct. You can edit the properties of style rules using the CSS panel or the CSS Rule definition dialog box.

Option 2: Correct. You can rename style rules to ensure that their names reflect the styles that they define.

Option 3: Incorrect. Style rules do not have extensions. Style rules can be contained in CSS or HTML files.

Option 4: Incorrect. You can edit properties for style rules but you cannot change the category that properties are in.

Correct answer(s):

1. Change the properties of style rules
2. Modify the names of style rules

SkillCheck

You are editing a web page and want to modify the fonts that are used in the headings. You decide to edit the style rule that defines the formatting of these headings.

Access the dialog box that enables you to modify a style rule and then change the font of the style rule named .style1 to Courier New, Courier, monospace.

Task:

1. Select the style rule that you want to edit.
2. Access the dialog box that enables you to edit the style rule.
3. Edit the style rule and accept the settings.

Answer

To complete the task

Step 1: Select *.style1* in the CSS Styles panel

Step 2: Click the **Edit Style** button

Step 3: Select **Courier New, Courier, monospace** from the Font drop-down list and click **OK**

3. Editing style sheets

External style sheets can contain large numbers of rules, so in some cases you might want to edit an entire style sheet instead of editing individual style rules.

Say you want to edit the style sheet Northglenn.css to modify the appearance of a web site.

To access the external style sheet, you double-click **Northglenn.css** on the CSS Styles panel.

The style sheet opens in a new document window, enabling you to edit the code to modify the style rules that it contains.

Code

```
.style1 {
font-family: "Times New Roman", Times, serif;
font-size: 24px;
color: #990000;
}
.style2 {
font-family: "Courier New", Courier, monospace;
```

```
font-size: 18px;
font-style: normal;
color: #000000;
}
tr {
border-top-width: medium;
border-right-width: medium;
```

You can access code hints to help you edit style rules.

To do this, you first position the cursor in the part of the code that you want to change. In this instance, you want to modify the color of .style2.

Graphic

The cursor is placed in the line of color code for .style2, in the following segment of code:

```
.style2 {
font-family:"Courier New", Courier, monospace;
font-size: 18px;
font-style:normal;
color: #000000;
}
```

You then press **Ctrl+Spacebar** and the code hint is shown. In this instance, the color picker is shown to help you select a color.

Note

*If you are using a Macintosh computer, you press **Command + Spacebar** to access code hints.*

You select a color from the color picker.

The hexadecimal code for the chosen color is automatically added to the document.

Graphic

The line of color code is now changed to

color: #999999;

Try It

Once you have finished editing the style rule, you can save the style sheet to apply the changes.

To complete the task

1. Select **File - Save As**

The Save As dialog box opens.

You click **Save** in the Save As dialog box to save the style sheet. This applies the changes you have made to the page that the style sheet is attached to.

You can remove a style sheet that is attached to a page using the CSS Styles panel.

To remove the Northglenn.css style sheet, for example, you first select **Northglenn.css** in the CSS Styles panel.

You then click the **Unlink CSS Stylesheet** button.

The style sheet has now been removed from the page.

SkillCheck

You are editing a web page and want to change its appearance by using different style rules. You decide first to remove the current styles that are applied to the page.

Remove the external style sheet, newstyles.css, from the current web page.

Task:

1. Select the external style sheet that you want to remove.
2. Remove the selected style sheet from the current page.

Answer

To complete the task

Step 1: Select **newstyles.css** in the CSS Styles panel

Step 2: Click the **Unlink CSS Stylesheet** button

Summary

The new Cascading Style Sheets (CSS) management features enable you to easily move CSS rules to different locations. You can move rules from one document to another, from the head of a document to an external style sheet, or between CSS files. Dreamweaver CS3 also enables you to convert inline styles to CSS styles, contained in the head of a document or in an external style sheet.

To change the appearance of a web page, you can edit CSS style rules. You can change the properties and the names of style rules.

You can also modify a web page by editing the external style sheet that is attached to it. You can modify and add or remove style rules from a style sheet. You can also remove an entire style sheet from a web page.

Working with CSS in Dreamweaver CS3

Learning Objective

After completing this topic, you should be able to

- *create, attach, and edit an external style sheet in a given scenario*

Exercise overview

In this exercise, you're required to use Cascading Style Sheets (CSS) to manage the appearance of a web page.

This involves the following tasks:

- creating an external style sheet
- attaching an external style sheet
- editing a style sheet

Task 1: Creating an external style sheet

You are creating a web site for the Northglenn Fitness Club, and your first task is to create a new CSS file that will be attached to all the pages that comprise the web site.

Create a new style sheet using the New Document dialog box. Then add a class style rule, named "style1," that will define a font size of 10.

Steps list
Instructions
1. Select **File - New**
2. Select **CSS** and then click the **Create** button
3. Click the **New CSS Rule** button on the CSS Styles tab
4. Type style1 in the Name text box and then click **OK**
5. Select **10** from the Size drop-down list and then click **OK**

Task 2: Attaching an external style sheet

You have finished creating the new external style sheet by defining various style rules and saving the CSS file. You now want to apply the style rules that you have created to the page that you are editing.

Attach the external style sheet, Northglenn.css, to the current page.

Steps list
Instructions
1. Click the **Attach Style Sheet** button on the CSS Styles panel
2. Click the **Browse** button
3. Select **Northglenn.css** and then click **OK**
4. Click **OK**

You have added the style sheet to the page that you are editing but now want to change one of its style rules to modify the appearance of a heading.

Use the appropriate dialog box to modify the .style1 rule contained in the Northglenn.css file so that the size is set to 16.

Steps list
Instructions
1. Select **.style1** on the CSS styles panel
2. Click the **Edit style** button
3. Select **16** from the Size drop-down list and then click **OK**

An external style sheet has been created, attached to a web page, and then edited.

CSS Layout Basics in Dreamweaver CS3

Learning Objective

After completing this topic, you should be able to

- *use design-time style sheets*

1. Identifying CSS box positions

Dreamweaver CS3 enables you to create the layout for web pages using CSS layout blocks.

A CSS-based layout requires less coding, which makes it easier to maintain than a table-based layout.

Layout blocks consist of web page elements that can be placed at any location on a page. Examples of layout blocks include div tags and layers – now more commonly referred to as absolutely positioned (AP) elements.

Using div tags, you can create boxes on a page and insert the required content into these boxes. Then you can position these boxes on the page, as desired. This method is known as the box model.

A box consists of a margin, border, padding, and content. You can set rules for each of these elements.

You can place boxes on a page using one of five different positions:

static

The static position enables you to place the box at its default position.

relative

The relative position enables you to place the box at its default location and to set the top and left positions of the box.

inherit

The inherit position enables you to set the box to use the properties of its parent box.

absolute

The absolute position enables you to place the box at a specific location on the page in relation to its parent box.

fixed

The fixed position enables you to place the box at a specific location on the page. The position of the box is defined in reference to the top-left corner of the page.

In addition to setting a position, you can set a box to float on a page by setting its float property.

You can choose to float the box on the left or the right.

Question

You are laying out a page using CSS, and have inserted a box 200 pixels from the top of the page. You have also placed another box inside the original box, and you want this inner box to be positioned 100 pixels from the top of the outer box.

Which box position should you select in this situation?

Options:

1. Absolute
2. Fixed
3. Inherit
4. Relative
5. Static

Answer

Option 1: Correct. The absolute position enables you to place the box at a specific location on the page. This will enable you to position the inner box 100 pixels from the top of the outer box.

Option 2: Incorrect. The fixed box position is used to position the box at a specified location that is defined in reference to the page.

Option 3: Incorrect. The inherit box position is used to set the box to use the properties of its parent box.

Option 4: Incorrect. The relative box position is used to set the top and left positions of the box and to place the box at its default location.

Option 5: Incorrect. The static box position is used to position the box at its default position.

Correct answer(s):

1. Absolute

Dreamweaver CS3 provides the Visual Aids feature, which enables you to track and identify the layout boxes on a page.

To use this feature, you first click the **Visual Aids** button on the Document toolbar.

Note

*Alternatively, you can select **View - Visual Aids** from the main menu.*

Three options on the **Visual Aids** enable you to work with CSS layouts.

CSS Layout Backgrounds

The **CSS Layout Backgrounds** option enables you to display the layout blocks in different background colors temporarily so you can differentiate between the layout blocks. These colors are configured by default and cannot be changed. The existing background color or background image disappears when you select this option.

CSS Layout Box Model

The **CSS Layout Box Model** option enables you to display the layout boxes with margins, borders, and padding. In addition, you can view the properties of a layout box as a tooltip when you move the mouse over the layout box.

CSS Layout Outlines

The **CSS Layout Outlines** option enables you to display layout blocks with dashed lines around their borders.

You can toggle the display of a visual aid on or off by selecting or deselecting it on the **Visual Aids** menu.

You can also hide all the visual aids by selecting **Hide All Visual Aids**.

Keyboard Sequence

*The keyboard alternative for hiding all the visual aids is **Ctrl+Shift+I**. On a Macintosh you press **Command+Shift+I**.*

Try It

Suppose you want to differentiate between the layout blocks on your web page by using colors.

To complete the task

1. Select **CSS Layout Backgrounds** from the **Visual Aids** menu

The background colors of the layout boxes on the web page have changed.

The layout boxes on the web page now appear in different background colors.

Question

You have inserted layout blocks and now want to view them in a way that displays their margins, borders, and padding.

Which visual aid option enables you to do this?

Options:

1. CSS Layout Backgrounds
2. CSS Layout Box Model
3. CSS Layout Outlines

Answer

Option 1: Incorrect. The CSS Layout Backgrounds visual aid enables you to view layout boxes in different background colors, rather than to view their margins, borders, and padding.

Option 2: Correct. The CSS Layout Box Model visual aid enables you to view margins, borders, and padding for the layout boxes. This visual aid also enables you to view the properties of a layout box as a tooltip when you move the mouse over the layout box.

Option 3: Incorrect. The CSS Layout Outlines visual aid enables you to view dashed lines around the layout boxes, rather than their margins, borders, and padding.

Correct answer(s):

2. CSS Layout Box Model

3. Laying out a page

To begin laying out a page using CSS, you can use design files. Design files are built-in templates that enable you to apply predefined layouts to new web pages you create.

Try It

To create a page with a CSS layout using a design file, you first open the New Document dialog box.

To complete the task

1. Select **File - New**
   Using keyboard: The keyboard alternative for opening the New Document dialog box is **Alt+F, N** or **Option+F, N** on a Macintosh.

The New Document dialog box opens.

In the New Document dialog box, you specify how you want a new document to be created.

Graphic

The New Document dialog box contains five category tabs – Blank Page, Blank Template, Page from Template, Page from Sample (default), and Other. Currently, the Page from Sample category is selected, so options for choosing a sample folder and page display.

You first select the **Blank Page** category to access options for creating a new page without using a template or a sample page.

With the Blank Page category selected, the New Document dialog box enables you to choose the page type you want to create and a predefined layout for the page.

Graphic

With the Blank Page category selected, the New Document dialog box displays Page Type and Layout list boxes, an HTML document preview box, DocType and Layout CSS drop-down list boxes, an Attach CSS file text box, and Help, Preferences, Create, and Cancel buttons.

In this case, you select **HTML** from the Page Type list box.

From the Layout list box, you can choose a predesigned CSS layout.

There are four types of layout options:

fixed

In a fixed layout type, the layout cannot be resized – either by the site visitor's text settings or by a browser. The width is specified in pixels.

elastic

In an elastic layout type, any columns can be resized by the site visitor, but not by the browser. The width is specified in a unit of measurement (ems) that is relative to the text size.

liquid

In a liquid layout type, columns can be resized by a browser, but not by the site visitor. Column width is specified as a percentage of the site visitor's browser size.

hybrid

In a hybrid layout type, the page width is a combination of the fixed, elastic, and liquid column types. For example, the layout may include both a fixed and elastic column type or a fixed and liquid column type.

In this case, you select **2 column elastic, left sidebar** from the Layout list box.

A preview of the layout you selected displays in the HTML document preview box.

Try It

Next you select a document type and a location for the layout's CSS. You decide to add the CSS for the layout to the head of the page you're creating.

To complete the task

1. Select **XHTML 1.1** from the DocType drop-down list

2. Ensure **Add to Head** is selected in the Layout CSS drop-down list and click **Create**

A new page is created with the specified CSS layout.

SkillCheck

Create an HTML page with a CSS layout using one liquid column centered on the page. Add the CSS for the layout to the head of the page you're creating.

You have already opened the New Document dialog box.

Task:

1. Choose the kind of page you want to create.
2. Choose the CSS layout you want to use.
3. Choose a location for the layout's CSS and create the page.

Answer

To complete the task

*Step 1: Select **HTML** from the Page Type list box*

*Step 2: Select **1 column liquid, centered** from the Layout list box*

*Step 3: Select **Add to Head** from the Layout CSS drop-down list and click **Create***

4. Using design-time style sheets

Dreamweaver CS3 enables you to use a style sheet and apply CSS styles when designing web pages. This type of style sheet is known as a design-time style sheet.

A design-time style sheet is available only when you are creating web pages in Dreamweaver – the styles are not visible once you preview the web page in a browser, although the browser displays the design or style associated with the web page.

You create a design-time style sheet the same way you create any other style sheet.

Suppose you want to display a background color for the selected box on a web page.

You type the code for the background color in the northglenn.css style sheet.

Graphic

You type the following code:
```
div#content {
background-color: #FFFFCC;
}
```

Try It

To apply the color, you must attach the style sheet to the web page.

To complete the task

1. Select **Text - CSS Styles - Design-time**
   Using keyboard: The keyboard alternative for attaching the style sheet to the web page is **Alt+T, C, D**. On a Macintosh, the alternative is **Option+T, C, D**.

The Design Time Style Sheets dialog box opens.

> The Design Time Style Sheets dialog box enables you to select a style sheet for your web page or hide a style sheet when creating the web page.

Graphic

The Design Time Style Sheets dialog box contains a Show only at design time pane and a Hide at design time pane, both with buttons for adding or removing style sheets. It also contains OK, Cancel, and Help buttons.

Try It

You decide to attach the northglenn.css style sheet to the current web page.

To complete the task

1. Click the **+** (plus sign) button above the Show only at design time pane
2. Select **northglenn** and click **OK**

The northglenn.css style sheet is listed in the Show only at design time pane.

> You click **OK** to close the dialog box.

> Dreamweaver CS3 enables you to use a design-time style sheet to display backgrounds, borders, or box models for non-CSS layout block elements, such as paragraphs and lists.

Try It

You want to display the paragraphs on your web page in orange as a CSS layout block. The code for the background color has been specified in the northglenn.css style sheet. You now need to use an attribute in the code to display the relevant block.

The Courseware Player cannot recognize input from your keyboard Enter key. Therefore, please click the Enter button provided instead of pressing the Enter key.

To complete the task

1. Type display:block; and press the **Enter** button provided

You have specified the display:block attribute for the paragraph page element.

Now when you view the web page in Design view, the paragraphs will appear as orange layout blocks.

SkillCheck

You have created a design-time style sheet, facilities.css, for the facilities.html web page. The style sheet and the web page are saved in the Northglenn2008 folder.

Attach the style sheet to the web page.

Task:

1. Open the Design Time Style Sheets dialog box.
2. Choose the option to display a CSS style sheet at design-time.
3. Select the CSS style sheet you want to attach and accept the selection.
4. Accept the settings and close the Design Time Style Sheets dialog box.

Answer

To complete the task

*Step 1: Select **Text - CSS Styles - Design-time***

*Step 2: Click the **+** (plus sign) button above the Show only at design time pane*

*Step 3: Select **facilities** and click **OK***

*Step 4: Click **OK** again*

Summary

Dreamweaver CS3 enables you to lay out web pages using Cascading Style Sheets (CSS) layout blocks. You can set the position for these boxes and configure them to float on web pages.

Dreamweaver CS3 also enables you to track and identify the layout boxes on a page using the Visual Aids feature.

You can use design files in Dreamweaver CS3 to apply predefined layouts to web pages you create. Using div tags, you can create boxes on a page and insert the required content in these boxes.

You can attach design-time style sheets to web pages to apply CSS styles when designing web pages. You can also use these style sheets to display backgrounds, borders, or box models for non-CSS layout blocks elements, such as paragraphs and lists.

CSS Positioning in Dreamweaver CS3

Learning Objectives

After completing this topic, you should be able to

   o   *recognize the CSS positioning properties*

○ *use div tags for layout*

1. CSS positioning properties

The final appearance of a web page is often determined simply by the order in which the page elements appear in the HTML code.

However, you can exert greater control over the positioning of elements by defining CSS positioning properties.

There are four types of positions that you can define using CSS:

absolute

Absolute positioning enables you to use coordinates to place content anywhere on your web page in relation to the closest positioned ancestor, or to the top left of the page if there is no ancestor.

relative

Relative positioning enables you to position content in relation to its position in the HTML code. When you assign a relative position to a tag, it is positioned relative to where it was placed originally.

static

Static positioning is the default HTML behavior and is managed using the normal flow of HTML.

fixed

Fixed positioning enables you to place elements at specific fixed positions in the browser window in relation to the top left corner of the page. Scrolling up or down has no effect on the positioning of these elements.

You can access the CSS positioning options for a style rule by opening the CSS Rule definition dialog box.

To do this, you select a style rule and then click the **Edit Style** button in the CSS Styles panel.

The options are available in the **Positioning** category.

Graphic

The CSS Rule definition dialog box has two main sections. The Category list box lists the categories that you can use to define style rules. The various options available for the selected category are also shown in the dialog box.

The options that you can configure using the Positioning category are

Type

The Type drop-down list enables you to specify the type of positioning that you want to apply to an element. You can choose absolute, fixed, relative, or static positioning.

Width and Height

The Width and Height drop-down lists enable you to specify the width and height of an element and the system of measurement used. The list also has an option that enables you to specify that the values should be set automatically.

Placement

The Placement section enables you to specify the placement and dimensions of an element. You can specify values for the top, right, bottom, and left of the element.

Visibility

The Visibility drop-down list enables you to specify whether an element must be visible or hidden on the web page.

Z-Index

The Z-Index drop-down list enables you to specify the depth of an element within layers. You can choose the auto option or specify a value.

Overflow

The Overflow drop-down list enables you to specify how an element should be displayed when a portion of it extends beyond the allocated space. The element can be visible, hidden, or scrollable.

Clip

The Clip section enables you to specify the visible portions of an element. You can specify values for the top, right, bottom, and left of the element.

Question

What properties can you set when defining CSS positioning rules?

Options:

1. Width and height
2. Overflow
3. Visibility
4. X-Index
5. Center point

Answer

Option 1: Correct. You can specify the width and height of an element and the system of measurement used.

Option 2: Correct. You can specify how an element displays when a portion of it extends beyond the allotted space.

Option 3: Correct. You can specify whether an element must be visible or hidden on your web page.

Option 4: Incorrect. You cannot define an X-Index for an element. You can define a Z-Index, which is used to determine the depth of an element within layers.

Option 5: Incorrect. You cannot set the center point of an element when positioning it. However, you can use the placement options to specify the placement and dimensions of an element.

Correct answer(s):

1. Width and height
2. Overflow
3. Visibility

44

Two of the most commonly used positioning elements are the div and span tags. A div tag is a block-level element, whereas a span tag is an inline element used to alter only a section of a layout element.

Both div and span tags can be used to style a specific section of a web page.

Div tags provide you with the flexibility to position most types of content anywhere on a web page. You can position them absolutely or relatively.

Provided you assign each div tag a unique ID, you can also create CSS rules to change the style and positioning of the div tags.

You want to use a div tag to style a specific section of text on your web page.

To begin, you select the text that you want to contain in the div tag.

Try It

You now want to insert the div tag.

To complete the task

1. Select **Insert - Layout Objects - Div Tag**
    Using keyboard: The keyboard alternative is **Alt+I, Y, D**. If you are using an Apple Macintosh, you select **Option+I, Y, D**.

The Insert Div Tag dialog box opens.

You can specify several options for inserting a div tag using the Insert Div Tag dialog box.

Graphic

The Insert Div Tag dialog box contains Insert, Class, and ID drop-down list boxes, and a New CSS Style button.

Insert

The Insert drop-down list enables you to specify the position of the div tag. You can place a tag at the insertion point, after the start, or before the end of a tag. If you have selected text, the **Wrap around text** option is selected by default.

Class

The Class drop-down list enables you to specify a class for the div tag. If you have attached a style sheet to the page, the classes in that style sheet will appear in the list.

ID

The ID drop-down list enables you to assign an ID to the div tag. If you have attached a style sheet to the page, the list displays the IDs defined in that style sheet.

New CSS Style

You can use the **New CSS Style** button to create a new CSS style for the div tag.

You choose to use the wrap around selection option, and assign the div tag a class and an ID.

Graphic

The Wrap around selection option is selected in the Insert drop-down list, style13 is selected in the Class drop-down list, and the text "retail" is entered in the ID drop-down list box.

You then click **OK** to accept the settings.

The div tag is inserted on the web page surrounding the selected text.

The text within the div tag is formatted using the style that was assigned to the tag.

When you move the pointer over the edge of a div tag, Dreamweaver highlights it so that it is more easily visible.

Graphic

The borders of the div tag are highlighted in red.

After adding a div tag to a page, you can edit it by modifying its properties.

To edit the div tag, you first select it in the Document window.

Graphic

The div tag is selected. The CSS Styles panel has three panes – Summary for Selection, About, and Properties. The defined properties for the selected style are listed in the Properties pane.

Try It

You want to change the font weight that is applied to the text contained in the div tag.

The font weight property for the div tag text is currently set to bold.

To complete the task

1.   Select **font-weight** in the Properties pane
2.   Click the down-pointing arrow that displays and select **normal** from the drop-down list

The style rule applied to the div tag is modified.

The font weight that is applied to the text in the div tag is modified and the changes are shown on the page.

You can use the CSS Styles panel to make further changes to the div tag's properties as needed.

SkillCheck

You want to use a div tag to style a block of text on a web page. You have already selected the text that you want to contain in the tag.
Use the menu bar to insert a new div tag. Specify the "style13" style and give the tag the ID "copyright."

Task:

1. Open the Insert Div Tag dialog box.
2. Specify the class style.
3. Assign the div tag an ID and then add it to the web page.

Answer

To complete the task

Step 1: *Select* ***Insert - Layout Objects - Div Tag***
Using keyboard: *The keyboard alternative is* ***Alt+I, Y, D****. On a Macintosh, the alternative is* ***Option+I, Y, D****.*

Step 2: *Select* ***style13*** *from the Class drop-down list*

Step 3: *Type* copyright *in the ID drop-down list box and click* ***OK***

3. Using absolute positioning

Absolute positioned (AP) elements are HTML page elements that have been assigned an absolute position.

You can create AP elements using any content that you can place in the body of an HTML document. For example, you can include text, images, or headings.

Dreamweaver enables you to use AP elements to lay out your web pages by

- o   placing AP elements in front of or behind each other

- o   hiding some AP elements while showing others

- o   moving AP elements across the screen

The most common type of AP element is an absolutely positioned div tag, but you can classify any HTML element as an AP element by assigning it an absolute position.

All AP elements that you add to a web page are listed in the AP Elements panel in the CSS panel group.

Graphic

The AP Elements panel lists all the AP elements on the page under two main columns – Name and Z.

You can add an AP element to your web page using the menu bar or the Layout category on the Insert bar.

Try It

You want to use the menu bar to add a new AP div tag.

To complete the task

1. Select **Insert - Layout Objects - AP Div**

The AP div tag is created and added to the page.

You can now add content within the AP div tag by clicking inside it and typing or inserting the content that you want it to contain.

You can create AP divs manually using the Draw AP Div feature.

To do this, you first click the **Draw AP Div** button in the Layout category on the Insert bar.

Graphic

The Layout category on the Insert bar has 15 buttons – Insert Div Tag, Draw AP Div, Spry Menu Bar, Spry Tabbed Panels, Spry Accordion, Spry Collapsible Panel, Table, Insert Row Above, Insert Row Below, Insert Column to the Left, Insert Column to the Right, IFrame, Frames, Draw Layout Table, and Draw Layout Cell.

You then position the cursor at the point on the page where you want to add the AP div tag.

To draw the AP div tag, you hold the mouse button and drag the cursor to another position on screen. When you release the mouse, the AP div tag is shown on your web page.

SkillCheck

You want to use an AP div tag to place a portion of content at an absolute position on a web page.

Use the menu bar to insert a new AP div tag on the web page.

Task:

1. Use the menu bar to add an AP div tag.

Answer

To complete the task

*Step 1: Select **Insert - Layout Objects - AP Div***

Summary

There are various Cascading Style Sheets (CSS) positioning properties that you can define to manage the layout and positioning of elements on your web pages. You can use absolute, relative, static, or fixed positioning.

A div tag is an HTML tag that can be used as a container for text, images, and other page elements. You can also assign div tags IDs and create CSS rules that define their style and positioning.

Absolute positioned (AP) elements are HTML page elements that have been assigned an absolute position.

The most common type of AP element is an absolutely positioned div tag. You can insert AP div tags using the menu bar or draw them manually.

Class and Advanced Style Rules in Dreamweaver CS3

Learning Objectives

After completing this topic, you should be able to

- *use class styles*
- *create an advanced style rule*
- *identify when you would apply advanced style rules*

1. Using class styles

Class style rules offer you greater control of document formatting than tag style rules.

When you create a tag style rule, Dreamweaver CS3 applies the same style rule to each instance of the tag in all documents using the style sheet.

With a class style rule, you can choose which tags to apply the style rule to. For example, you can create a style rule that underlines text and makes it red. You can then apply it to multiple tags, such as list tags, heading tags, and paragraph tags.

In Design view, you can apply a class style rule by selecting the text you want to format and choosing the required style from the Style drop-down list on the Property inspector.

In Code view, you can use a class attribute to apply a class style rule to a tag. For example, you can add a class attribute directly to a <p> tag.

Code

```
<p class="underlineit">Reasons for joining Northglenn Fitness Club: </p>
```

If you want to add a class style rule to an individual word or words, you can enclose the text in <span> tags and add a class attribute.

Code

```
<p>No waiting around! The gym has <span class="underlineit">250</span> machines, each with a personal TV.
</p>
```

The class attribute always takes the name of the class style rule as its value.

You can configure a class style rule from Design view or add it directly to an external or embedded Cascading Style Sheet (CSS). The class style rule name is defined first, followed by its associated style rules, which are included within curly braces and separated by semicolons.

Code

49

```
.underlineit {
color: #FF0000;
text-decoration: underline;
}
```

The name of a class style rule definition must always begin with a period followed by an alphabetical character. The period, which is required in the style sheet only, enables the CSS parser to distinguish a class style rule from a selector style rule.

Code

```
.underlineit {
color: #FF0000;
text-decoration: underline;
}
```

When creating class styles through the interface, Dreamweaver automatically inserts the period in the class name.

The class style name should not contain spaces, additional punctuation, or special characters. It is a good idea to name the class style rule according to its function, for example ".underlineit."

Code

```
.underlineit {
color: #FF0000;
text-decoration: underline;
}
```

If you want to limit a class style rule to a particular element, you include the element before the period in the class name. This enables you to create special styles for certain instances of an element.

Code

```
p.underlineit {
color: #FF0000;
text-decoration: underline;
}
```

Try It

To define style rules using Design view, you need to open the New CSS Rule dialog box.

To complete the task

1. Click the **New CSS Rule** button at the bottom of the CSS Styles panel

You can now create a class style rule.

Try It

Suppose you want to add a class style rule that bolds text and colors it dark red to the northglenn.css style sheet.

The New CSS Rule dialog box has three main options: Selector Type, Tag, and Define in. The Selector Type option has three radio buttons: Class (can apply to any tag), Tag (redefines the look of a specific tag), and Advanced (ID's, psuedo-class selectors). The Define in section has two radio buttons: (New Style Sheet File) and This document only.

To complete the task

1. Select the **Class (can apply to any tag)** radio button in the Selector Type section
2. Type boldit in the Name text box and click **OK**

Dreamweaver CS3 opens the CSS Rule definition for .boldit dialog box, where you can make your style selections.

You select **bold** from the Weight drop-down list.

You specify the red color using the color picker or by typing the hexadecimal value in the Color text box.

Graphic

The value #990000 is entered in the Color text box.

You click **OK** to confirm your choices and create the class style rule.

Dreamweaver CS3 adds the class style rule to the CSS Styles panel.

You can open the style sheet to examine the CSS code for the new class style rule.

Code

```
.boldit {
 font-weight: bold;
 color: #990000;
}
```

Now suppose you want to use a class style rule to format specific content in a document.

You can select **Text - CSS Styles** from the main menu, or you can use the Style drop-down list on the Property inspector, to apply or remove class styles.

Try It

Suppose you decide to use the Style drop-down list to apply the .boldit class style rule to a paragraph. First you position your cursor within the paragraph.

To complete the task

1. Select **boldit** from the Style drop-down list

Dreamweaver CS3 applies the class style rule to the text.

51

In Code view, you can verify that Dreamweaver CS3 has added a class attribute to the paragraph <p> tag. The value of the class attribute is the name of the class style rule.

Graphic

The code for the paragraph tag is now:
<p class="boldit"><font size="2" face="Verdana, Arial, Helvetica, sans-serif">Reasons for
joining Northglenn
Fitness Club: </font></p>

Try It

Now you decide that you want to remove the class style rule from the paragraph. You ensure the cursor is within the paragraph.

To complete the task

1. Select **None** from the Style drop-down list

Dreamweaver CS3 removes the class style rule.

In Code view, you can verify that Dreamweaver CS3 has removed the class attribute from the paragraph tag.

Graphic

The code for the paragraph tag is now:
<p><font size="2" face="Verdana, Arial, Helvetica, sans-serif">Reasons for
joining Northglenn
Fitness Club: </font></p>

You cannot click a class style rule in the CSS Style panel to remove it from content – it does not act like a toggle.

Instead, you need to use the Style drop-down list on the Property inspector or the **Text** menu.

Or you can position the cursor in the styled text, right-click, and select **CSS Styles - None** from the shortcut menu that displays.

SkillCheck

Create a new class style called ".italics" that italicizes text.

Task:

1. Access options for creating a class style.
2. Specify that you want to create a class style.
3. Specify a name for the new class style and create the style.
4. Add a class style rule that italicizes text.

Answer

To complete the task

*Step 1: Click the **New CSS Rule** button*

*Step 2: Select the **Class (can apply to any tag)** radio button*

*Step 3: Type italics in the Name text box and click **OK***

*Step 4: Select **italic** from the Style drop-down list and click **OK***

2. Applying advanced style rules

Advanced style rules in Dreamweaver CS3 enable you to specify styles for

- content that has different states, such as hyperlinks

- the first line or the first letter of a paragraph

- a group of tags

- a tag that occurs in a particular context

Tag and class style rules are easy to apply to elements because the tags can be found in the CSS Styles All Rules pane. The All Rules tree simply displays your styles in a tree-like structure.

However, some publishing preferences – such as having a specific style for the first letter of a paragraph – are more difficult to apply. For example, the All Rules pane does not contain an element that identifies the first letter of a paragraph.

Dreamweaver CS3 enables you to use selectors to select and apply style rules to elements that lie outside the All Rules pane.

A selector is a simple pattern-matching rule used to determine which content a style rule should be applied to.

For example, H1 is the selector in this CSS code

```
H1 {
  font-family: sans-serif;
}
```

The selector may be a simple element name or a complex contextual pattern. When all conditions of the pattern are met, the content is selected and the style rule is applied.

For example, td p is the selector in this CSS code

```
td p{
  font-size: 14px;
}
```

Dreamweaver CS3 supports selectors through the use of pseudo-classes, group selectors, and contextual selectors.

Note

Pseudo-classes enable you to add special effects to some selectors.

Dreamweaver CS3 contains four preset pseudo-classes, each of which enables you to select a particular state for a link.

The anchor pseudo-classes are

a:active

You use the a:active pseudo-class to specify the state of a link when a user selects it in a browser.

By default, it is colored red.

a:hover

You use the a:hover pseudo-class to specify the state of a link when a user rolls over it in a browser.

a:link

You use the a:link pseudo-class to specify the state of a link before a user interacts with it – that is, before it has been selected, rolled over, or visited.

By default, it is colored blue.

a:visited

You use the a:visited pseudo-class to specify the state of a link after a user has clicked and followed it.

By default, it is colored purple.

In addition to the anchor pseudo-classes, Dreamweaver CS3 accepts pseudo-elements for adding special effects to characters, including

Graphic

Examples of code using pseudo-elements are

p.summary:first-line {
font-family: Arial, Helvetica, sans-serif;
color: #990000;
}

p.summary:first-letter {
font-family: Arial, Helvetica, sans-serif;
font-size: 16px;
}

:first-line

The :first-line pseudo-element enables you to select and apply a style to the first line of content contained in a specific tag. For example, if you want to select the first line of a paragraph, you use p.summary:first-line.

:first-letter

The :first-letter pseudo-element enables you to select and apply a style to the first letter of content contained in a specific tag. For example, if you want to select the first letter of a paragraph, you use p.summary:first-letter.

The anchor pseudo-classes are more widely supported than the :first-line and :first-letter pseudo-elements.

Many browsers accept pseudo-elements, but render them in slightly different ways.

The final types of selectors accepted by Dreamweaver CS3 are

group selectors

You use a group selector to apply the same style rule to a group of tags.

For example, to apply the same style rule to parent paragraph, table definition, and list item elements, you use p, td, li, as in this code

p, td, li{color:#006400;}.

contextual selectors

You use a contextual selector to apply a single style rule to a tag that is nested within another tag. Contextual selectors enable you automatically to override the style rules that a nested tag inherits from its parent.

For example, to apply a strong style to text only when it is within a parent paragraph tag, which is in turn within a parent table definition tag, you use td p strong, as in this code

td p strong{color:#990000;}.

You should use group selectors only when you want to apply the same style to multiple tags.

You cannot use a group selector to apply a set of common styles for the group and then use individual tag style rules to define extra properties. With CSS, you cannot define multiple styles for the same HTML tag.

For example, if you define a group selector such as body blockquote p, you cannot define another style rule for the body, blockquote, or p tags.

Because contextual selectors select an element within a given context, you can create other individual tag style rules for each of the tags used to describe the context.

For example, if you define a contextual selector such as body blockquote p, you can define other style rules for the <body>, <blockquote>, and <p> tags.

Question

Advanced style rules in Dreamweaver CS3 enable you to specify style rules for elements not directly referenced in the document tree.

Identify the scenarios in which you would apply advanced style rules.

Options:

1. For a group of tags where a tag style rule already exists for each tag
2. To apply a single style rule to a tag
3. For content that has different states
4. For the first line or the first letter of a paragraph

Answer

Option 1: Incorrect. Dreamweaver CS3 enables you to use a group selector – p,td,li, for example – to apply the same style rule to a group of tags. However, once you have defined a tag style rule, that tag cannot appear in a group selector. With CSS, you cannot define multiple styles for the same HTML tag.

Option 2: Incorrect. You can use a contextual selector – td p strong, for example – to apply a single style rule to a tag that is nested within another tag.

Option 3: Correct. Dreamweaver CS3 provides four preset anchor pseudo-classes that you can use to define style rules for links in various states. The anchor pseudo-classes are a:active, a:hover, a:link, and a:visited.

Option 4: Correct. Dreamweaver CS3 supports the first-line and first-letter pseudo-classes to enable you to select the first line and the first letter of content contained in a specific tag, such as a paragraph tag <p>.

Correct answer(s):

3. For content that has different states
4. For the first line or the first letter of a paragraph

3. Creating advanced style rules

Suppose you want to use a CSS selector to change the appearance of the links on a web page.

You click the **New CSS Rule** button at the bottom of the CSS Styles panel to open the New CSS Rule dialog box.

Try It

You want to change the color of a link in its normal state – blue by default – to dark green (#006400). So you define an advanced style rule and add it to the current style sheet attached to the document.

The New CSS Rule dialog box is open. There are three main sections: Selector Type, Name, and Define in.

To complete the task

1. Select the **Advanced (IDs, pseudo-class selectors)** radio button in the Selector Type section
2. Select **a:link** from the Selector drop-down list and click **OK**

The CSS Rule definition for a:link dialog box opens.

You specify the color – in this case by entering the hexadecimal value in the Color text box – and you click **OK**.

Graphic

The Type section on the CSS Rule definition for a:link dialog box has nine options: Font, Size, Style, Line height, Decoration, Weight, Variant, Case, and Color.

Note

You can select the four anchor styles from the Selector drop-down list in the New CSS Rule dialog box. However, if you want to create
a :first-line, :first-letter, group, or contextual selector, you must type the selector name into the Selector drop-down list box.

Dreamweaver applies the style to the document.

And it adds the style to the CSS Styles panel.

There is no visible change to the HTML code.

You open the style sheet to examine the code for the advanced style rule.

Graphic

The code is:

a:link (color: #006400;)

Although you can preview the new color in Dreamweaver CS3, you cannot preview a hover color in Dreamweaver. You must preview it in a browser.

To preview it, you click the **Preview/Debug in browser** button and select your default browser option, in this case **Preview in Iexplore**.

When the web page opens, you verify that the default color for the link is dark green.

Now suppose that you have set the color for the link to change to light green when you hover your cursor over it.

Then when you roll over the link, it changes to light green as expected.

SkillCheck

Create an advanced style rule to change the color of links so that they display in the bright green color with the hexadecimal value #00FF00 when users roll over the links. To identify the required color, type its value.

Task:

1. Open the New CSS Rule dialog box.
2. Specify that you want to create an advanced style rule.
3. Specify the state of a link when a user rolls over it in a browser and accept the change.
4. Enter the hexadecimal color value and apply the style to the document.

Answer

To complete the task

Step 1: *Click the* **New CSS Rule** *button*

Step 2: *Select* **Advanced (IDs, pseudo-class selectors)** *in the Selector Type section*

Step 3: *Select* **a:hover** *from the Selector drop-down list and click* **OK**

Step 4: *Type #00FF00 in the Color text box and click* **OK**

Summary

You can use class style rules to apply the same style rule to multiple tags. You can apply them to all or some of the content in an element.

You can use the Property inspector, menu options, or the CSS Styles panel to apply or remove class styles.

You can use advanced style rules to specify styles for content that has different states, for the first line or letter of a paragraph, for a group of tags, or for tags that occur in particular contexts.

To create an advanced style rule, you specify the rule type and a selector, and then define the rule.

Applying Advanced CSS in Dreamweaver CS3

Learning Objective

After completing this topic, you should be able to

- *apply advanced CSS techniques to a web page*

Exercise overview

In this exercise, you're required to apply advanced Cascading Style Sheets (CSS) techniques to a web page.

This involves the following tasks:

- laying out a web page
- creating a div tag
- creating an advanced style rule

Task 1: Laying out a web page

You need to design a web page for Northglenn Fitness Club. Before you add content to the page, you want to manage its layout. You decide to use one of Dreamweaver's built-in templates to do this.

Create an HTML page with a CSS layout containing one fixed column centered on the page.

Add the CSS that will define the layout of your web page to the head of the page you're creating. You've already opened the New Document dialog box.

Steps list
Instructions
1. Select **HTML** from the Template Type list box
2. Select **1 column fixed, centered** from the Layout list box
3. Select **Add to Head** from the Layout CSS drop-down list and click **Create**

Task 2: Creating a div tag

You have added some text to your web page and now want to position and style a section of it. You decide to use CSS to achieve the formatting that you want.

Use the menu bar to insert a new div tag. Select the class style named "style13" and assign the tag the ID "list."

You have already selected the text that you want to wrap in the div tag.

Steps list
Instructions
1. Select **Insert - Layout Objects - Div Tag**
2. Select **style13** from the Class drop-down list
3. Type list in the ID text box and click **OK**

Task 3: Creating an advanced style rule

You want to change certain aspects of the page that you have designed by creating an advanced style rule.

Create a new advanced style rule that defines a font weight of bold for links that have been visited.

Steps list
Instructions
1. Click the **New CSS Rule** button
2. Select **Advanced (IDs, pseudo-class selectors)** in the Selector Type section
3. Select **a:visited** from the Selector drop-down list and click **OK**
4. Select **bold** from the Weight drop-down list and click **OK**

An HTML page with a CSS layout has been created, a div tag has been inserted, and an advanced style rule has been created.

Ajax, XML, and CSS

Learning Objectives

After completing this topic, you should be able to

- *use the XMLHttpRequest object to retrieve an XML document from a server*
- *extract element and attribute values from an XML document and add them to a page*
- *use CSS with Ajax to apply a style dynamically*

1. Creating and retrieving XML documents

Ajax applications can retrieve and display information from web servers asynchronously. This information may be stored in either text or XML format. However, most developers use XML because it is more structured and allows easy identification and organization of data.

You can use the predefined JavaScript object, XMLHttpRequest, to retrieve XML data. This object contains multiple methods and properties that allow you to efficiently interact with web servers and asynchronously download data.

Suppose you're creating an Ajax-based web site for a fitness club, NorthGlenn Fitness. The club offers five membership options. You want to allow prospective customers to register for these options online.

When registering online, prospective customers should be able to view details about the different membership options at the click of a button. So that these details are retrieved quickly, you decide to store them in an XML document named memberships.xml.

Before you start creating your XML document, you should be able to identify its basic components.

These components include

Code

```xml
<?xml version="1.0"?>
<PrimaryTag>
  <SecondTag attributeX="2">
    <InnerMostTag>Text</InnerMostTag>
    <br/>
  </SecondTag>
</PrimaryTag>
```

type definition

Each XML document starts with a type definition. This definition distinguishes the XML document from other types of files.

version declaration

In the first line of an XML document, you also declare the XML version you're using.

tags

You enclose the contents of an XML document within pairs of opening and closing tags. You should ensure that each tag pair is correctly nested. For example, the innermost opening tag in a set of nested tag pairs should match the innermost closing tag. You can also have empty tags, such as the <br/> tag. These tags don't require any content.

elements, and

Each tag pair and its contents constitute an element. Each XML document contains a main – or primary – element that encloses all the other elements.

attributes

To specify the properties of an XML element, you use an attribute. You must enclose all attribute values within quotation marks.

Tags are the most important components of an XML document. Although you have the flexibility to create and customize the tags, there are certain restrictions you should observe when naming them.

For example, you should be aware that tag names are case sensitive. Also, when naming a tag, you should

Code

```
<?xml version="1.0"?>
<PrimaryTag>
  <SecondTag attributeX="2">
    <InnerMostTag>Text</InnerMostTag>
    <br/>
  </SecondTag>
</PrimaryTag>
```

- use either a letter or an underscore as the first character

- use alphanumeric characters, underscores, periods, or hyphens as the second and subsequent characters

- exclude spaces, any other punctuation marks, and special characters, such as parentheses and brackets, and

- avoid using keywords

You're now creating the memberships.xml document.

Code

```
<?xml version="1.0"?>

     <                    >



     <        >
<membership            >
  <name>Full Off-Peak</name>
```

61

```
        <month>$75</month>
        <join>$300</join>
    </membership>
    <membership>
        <name>Fitness Only</name>
        <month>$60</month>
        <join>$250</join>
    </membership>
    <membership>
        <name>Family</name>
        <month>$250</month>
        <join>$1000</join>
    </membership>
```

The memberships *tag pair forms the primary element in the document.*

Details about each membership option are enclosed within membership *tags.*

The name *tags enclose the name of each membership option, the* join *tags enclose the option's joining fee, and the* month *tags, the monthly fee.*

To signify the type of each membership option, you assign an attribute named type *to the* membership *tags. The* type *attribute can take two values –* unlimited *and* off-peak.

To ensure the quality and validity of memberships.xml, you can record the applicable restrictions and rules in a *Document Type Definition*, or DTD, document. A DTD is also known as an *XML schema*.

An XML schema provides the following details:

Graphic

An XML schema contains the following type of code:

```
<?xml version="1.0" encoding="utf-8"?>
<xs:schema attributeFormDefault="unqualified" elementFormDefault="qualified"
xmlns:xs="http://www.w3.org/2001/XMLSchema">
 <xs:element name="memberships">
  <xs:complexType>
   <xs:sequence>
    <xs:element minOccurs="0" maxOccurs="unbounded" name="membership">
     <xs:complexType>
      <xs:sequence>
       <xs:element minOccurs="0" name="name" type="xs:string" />
       <xs:element minOccurs="0" name="join" type="xs:string" />
       <xs:element minOccurs="0" name="month" type="xs:string" />
      </xs:sequence>
      <xs:attribute name="type" type="xs:string" use="optional" />
```

```
        </xs:complexType>
      </xs:element>
    </xs:sequence>
  </xs:complexType>
 </xs:element>
</xs:schema>
```

- the sequence in which elements should appear in an XML document

- the attributes each element can have

- the data format each element can contain, and

- the maximum number of times each element can be reused in the document

You've already created a schema and stored the memberships.xml document on a web server. To allow users to download data from this document, you now add the **Show Membership Options** button to the NorthGlenn Fitness home page.

Graphic

The following code adds the Show Membership Options button:

<input type="button" value="Show Membership Options" onclick="loadXML()" />

Code

```
<!DOCTYPE html PUBLIC "-//W3C//DTD XHTML 1.0 Transitional//EN"
  "http://www.w3.org/TR/xhtml1/DTD/xhtml1-transitional.dtd">
<html xmlns="http://www.w3.org/1999/xhtml">
 <head>
  <meta http-equiv="Content-Type" content="text/html";
    charset="iso8859-1" />
  <title>Northglenn Fitness Club | Membership</title>
  <script type="text/javascript" language="Javascript">
  </script>
 </head>
 <body>
  <h2>Membership Packages</h2>
  <div id="XML"></div>
  <form>
  <input type="button" value="Show Membership Options"
    onclick="loadXML()" />
  </form>
 </body>
</html>
```

When a user clicks the button, the loadXML() function is triggered. You want this function to create an XMLHttpRequest instance that requests and retrieves the memberships.xml document.

Graphic

The loadXML() function is assigned to the onclick event.

Code

```
<!DOCTYPE html PUBLIC "-//W3C//DTD XHTML 1.0 Transitional//EN"
  "http://www.w3.org/TR/xhtml1/DTD/xhtml1-transitional.dtd">
<html xmlns="http://www.w3.org/1999/xhtml">
 <head>
  <meta http-equiv="Content-Type" content="text/html";
   charset="iso8859-1" />
  <title>Northglenn Fitness Club | Membership</title>
  <script type="text/javascript" language="Javascript">
  </script>
 </head>
 <body>
  <h2>Membership Packages</h2>
  <div id="XML"></div>
  <form>
  <input type="button" value="Show Membership Options"
   onclick="loadXML()" />
  </form>
 </body>
</html>
```

You're now configuring the loadXML() function.

You first ensure that this function can create an instance of the XMLHttpRequest object for Mozilla-based browsers. Then, for Microsoft Internet Explorer browsers, you implement this object as an ActiveXObject.

Graphic

The code for the loadXML function is

```
function loadXML()
{
 if (window.XMLHttpRequest)
 {
  ajaxObject = new XMLHttpRequest();
 } else if (window.ActiveXObject)
 {
  ajaxObject = new ActiveXObject("Microsoft.XMLHTTP");
 }
}
```

Code

```
   charset="iso8859-1" />
  <title>Northglenn Fitness Club | Membership</title>
  <script type="text/javascript" language="Javascript">
  var ajaxObject = null;
  function loadXML()
```

```
    {
    if (window.XMLHttpRequest)
    {
      ajaxObject = new XMLHttpRequest();
    } else if (window.ActiveXObject)
    {
      ajaxObject = new ActiveXObject("Microsoft.XMLHTTP");
    }
    }
  </script>
</head>
<body>
  <h2>Membership Packages</h2>
  <div id="XML"></div>
  <form>
  <input type="button" value="Show Membership Options"
    onclick="loadXML()" />
  </form>
</body>
</html>
```

Next you add code to override any errors.

Graphic

The code for this is

```
if (ajaxObject.overrideMimeType)
{
 ajaxObject.overrideMimeType("text/xml");
}
```

Code

```
    function loadXML()
    {
    if (window.XMLHttpRequest)
    {
      ajaxObject = new XMLHttpRequest();
    } else if (window.ActiveXObject)
    {
      ajaxObject = new ActiveXObject("Microsoft.XMLHTTP");
    }
    if (ajaxObject.overrideMimeType)
    {
      ajaxObject.overrideMimeType("text/xml");
    }
    }
  </script>
</head>
<body>
  <h2>Membership Packages</h2>
  <div id="XML"></div>
```

```
    <form>
    <input type="button" value="Show Membership Options"
      onclick="loadXML()" />
    </form>
  </body>
</html>
```

If the XMLHttpRequest instance exists, you want to use it to retrieve the memberships.xml document from the server. So you add an if statement to check whether the required instance has been created.

Graphic

The code to verify whether the XMLHttpRequest instance exists is

if (ajaxObject)

Code

```
    ajaxObject = new XMLHttpRequest();
    } else if (window.ActiveXObject)
    {
    ajaxObject = new ActiveXObject("Microsoft.XMLHTTP");
    }
    if (ajaxObject.overrideMimeType)
    {
    ajaxObject.overrideMimeType("text/xml");
    }
    if (ajaxObject)
    {

    }
    }
  </script>
 </head>
 <body>
  <h2>Membership Packages</h2>
  <div id="XML"></div>
  <form>
  <input type="button" value="Show Membership Options"
    onclick="loadXML()" />
  </form>
 </body>
</html>
```

In the if statement, you then add the open() method. This method enables the XMLHttpRequest instance to communicate with the server.

To the open() method, you pass on the HTTP method, GET, which can retrieve documents. You also pass on the path to the required document. And to specify asynchronous processing, you pass on the Boolean value true.

Graphic

---

ajaxObject.open("GET", "memberships.xml", true);

Code

```
    ajaxObject = new XMLHttpRequest();
  } else if (window.ActiveXObject)
  {
    ajaxObject = new ActiveXObject("Microsoft.XMLHTTP");
  }
  if (ajaxObject.overrideMimeType)
  {
    ajaxObject.overrideMimeType("text/xml");
  }
  if (ajaxObject)
  {
    ajaxObject.open("GET", "memberships.xml", true);
  }
}
</script>
</head>
<body>
  <h2>Membership Packages</h2>
  <div id="XML"></div>
  <form>
  <input type="button" value="Show Membership Options"
    onclick="loadXML()" />
  </form>
</body>
</html>
```

Note

If you don't pass on any Boolean *value to the* open() *method, it processes all server requests and responses asynchronously. To enforce synchronous processing, you need to set the* Boolean *value to* false.

To process the responses sent by the server, you assign the function, displayXML(), to the onreadystatechange event. Each time this event fires, the function is called. And to ensure the GET request is sent to the server, you configure the send() method.

Graphic

The code to pass on the displayXML() function is:

ajaxObject.onreadystatechange = displayXML;

And the code to configure the send() method is

ajaxObject.send(null);

```
      {
        ajaxObject = new ActiveXObject("Microsoft.XMLHTTP");
      }
      if (ajaxObject.overrideMimeType)
      {
        ajaxObject.overrideMimeType("text/xml");
      }
      if (ajaxObject)
      {
        ajaxObject.open("GET", "memberships.xml", true);
        ajaxObject.onreadystatechange = displayXML;
        ajaxObject.send(null);
      }
    }
  </script>
 </head>
 <body>
  <h2>Membership Packages</h2>
  <div id="XML"></div>
  <form>
  <input type="button" value="Show Membership Options"
    onclick="loadXML()" />
  </form>
 </body>
</html>
```

In the displayXML function, you first ensure that the document is fully downloaded by making sure that the readyState property is equal to 4. This indicates that the request has finished and that the response is ready. The entire XML data in the document is now stored as a read-only object in the responseXML property. This property belongs to the XMLHttpRequest object.

Graphic

The code to do this is

```
    if (ajaxObject.readyState == 4)
```

Code

```
   if (ajaxObject)
   {
     ajaxObject.open("GET", "memberships.xml", true);
     ajaxObject.onreadystatechange = displayXML;
     ajaxObject.send(null);
   }
  }
  function displayXML()
  {
   if (ajaxObject.readyState == 4)
   {
```

```
      }
    }
  </script>
</head>
<body>
  <h2>Membership Packages</h2>
  <div id="XML"></div>
  <form>
  <input type="button" value="Show Membership Options"
    onclick="loadXML()" />
  </form>
</body>
</html>
```

To ensure the XML data can be used, you then pass on the object stored in the responseXML property to a variable named xmlData.

Graphic

The code to do this is

> *var xmlData = ajaxObject.responseXML;*

Code

```
    if (ajaxObject)
    {
      ajaxObject.open("GET", "memberships.xml", true);
      ajaxObject.onreadystatechange = displayXML;
      ajaxObject.send(null);
    }
  }
  function displayXML()
  {
    if (ajaxObject.readyState == 4)
    {
      var xmlData = ajaxObject.responseXML;
    }
  }
  </script>
</head>
<body>
  <h2>Membership Packages</h2>
  <div id="XML"></div>
  <form>
  <input type="button" value="Show Membership Options"
    onclick="loadXML()" />
  </form>
</body>
</html>
```

Finally, you configure an alert message to be displayed as soon as the download completes.

Graphic

The code to do this is

alert("XML Document downloaded");

Code

```
    {
      ajaxObject.open("GET", "memberships.xml", true);
      ajaxObject.onreadystatechange = displayXML;
      ajaxObject.send(null);
    }
  }
  function displayXML()
  {
    if (ajaxObject.readyState == 4)
    {
      var xmlData = ajaxObject.responseXML;
      alert("XML Document downloaded");
    }
  }
 </script>
</head>
<body>
 <h2>Membership Packages</h2>
 <div id="XML"></div>
 <form>
 <input type="button" value="Show Membership Options"
   onclick="loadXML()" />
 </form>
</body>
</html>
```

Question

The content for one of the sections on your Ajax web page is stored in the address.xml file. You want the web page to asynchronously retrieve this content from the web server.

What should you do to ensure this?

Code

```
  <script type="text/javascript" language="Javascript">
  var obj = null;
  function retrieveXML()
  {
   if (window.XMLHttpRequest)
   {
     obj = new XMLHttpRequest();
   } else if (window.ActiveXObject)
   {
     obj = new ActiveXObject("Microsoft.XMLHTTP");
```

```
    }

    // additional code

    {
      obj.open("address.xml");

    // additional code

    }
```

Options:

1. Configure the open() method to override all errors
2. Assign the Boolean value false to the open() method
3. Pass on the data in address.xml, once it's been downloaded, to the obj instance
4. Send a GET method to the server if the obj instance exists

Answer

Option 1: This option is incorrect. You only use the open() *method to ensure that an* XMLHttpRequest *object can communicate with a web server. You should configure the code to override errors separately.*

Option 2: This option is incorrect. You want to ensure asynchronous retrieval of the content. So you should set the Boolean *value to* true, *not* false.

Option 3: This option is incorrect. After download, the data is automatically stored in the responseXML *property of the* obj *instance. However, the data is in read-only format. If you want to use the data, you need to transfer it to another variable.*

Option 4: This option is correct. To retrieve the XML file, you need to use the GET method in conjunction with the open() *method. Since the* open() *method belongs to the* obj *instance, you can use the GET method only if the instance exists.*

Correct answer(s):

4. Send a GET method to the server if the obj instance exists

2. Adding XML data to a web page

You've configured the NorthGlenn Fitness web site to download the memberships.xml document. You now want to extract the saved XML data and add it to a web page using JavaScript.

You can use various techniques to extract XML data with JavaScript. One of these techniques is to configure the JavaScript code to access and retrieve nodes from an XML file. These nodes are simply the XML elements.

You categorize the primary element in an XML file as the root node and the other elements as child nodes.

Code

```xml
<?xml version="1.0"?>
<memberships>
  <membership type="unlimited">
    <name>Full</name>
    <month>$105</month>
    <join>$450</join>
  </membership>
  <membership type="off-peak">
    <name>Full Off-Peak</name>
    <month>$75</month>
    <join>$300</join>
  </membership>
  <membership>
    <name>Fitness Only</name>
    <month>$60</month>
    <join>$250</join>
  </membership>
  <membership>
    <name>Family</name>
    <month>$250</month>
    <join>$1000</join>
  </membership>
</memberships>
```

The child nodes also follow a hierarchy. All the nodes within a child node are its children. And all the child nodes at the same level are siblings. In the example, the name, month, and join nodes are siblings. All the membership nodes are also siblings.

Graphic

The name element consists of the following tag pair:
<name>
</name>

And its sibling, the month element, includes the following pair:

<month>
</month>

Code

```xml
<?xml version="1.0"?>
<memberships>
  <membership type="unlimited">
    <name>Full</name>
    <month>$105</month>
    <join>$450</join>
  </membership>
  <membership type="off-peak">
    <name>Full Off-Peak</name>
```

```
      <month>$75</month>
      <join>$300</join>
   </membership>
   <membership>
      <name>Fitness Only</name>
      <month>$60</month>
      <join>$250</join>
   </membership>
   <membership>
      <name>Family</name>
      <month>$250</month>
      <join>$1000</join>
   </membership>
</memberships>
```

To retrieve the nodes, you use the built-in node properties of JavaScript.

These properties include

documentElement

You use the documentElement property to extract the root node from an XML document.

childNodes

The childNodes property enables you to extract all the child nodes from the currently active node.

firstChild

With the firstChild property, you can extract the first child node from an XML document. This child node belongs to the node that is currently active.

lastChild

Using the lastChild property, you can extract the last child node from the currently active node.

nextSibling, and

If you want to extract the next sibling of the currently active node, you use the nextSibling property.

previousSibling

To extract the node that immediately precedes the currently active node, you use the previousSibling property.

Another useful node property is the nodeType property.

According to the *Document Object Model*, or DOM, an XML document can have 12 different node types. You determine the node type based on its value. For a given node, the nodeType property stores this value.

Graphic

The table lists the value associated with each node type. It consists of two columns – one for the values and the other for the associated node types. There are 12 rows in the table. The rows indicate that value 1 is associated with element nodes, value 2 with attribute nodes, value 3 with text, value 4 with CDATA, or character data, sections, value 5 with XML entity references, value 6 with XML entities, value 7 with XML processing instructions, value 8 with XML comments,

JavaScript provides two other properties that extract details about a node – nodeName and nodeValue. You use nodeName to extract the name of the node and nodeValue to extract its value.

Suppose you want a NorthGlenn Fitness web page to extract and display the joining fee for each type of membership. To do this, you add the join_fee() function to the web page.

Code

```
function join_fee(xmlData)
{

}
```

To access the joining fee details saved in the join node of xmlData, the web page first needs to pass through the root node, memberships. To enable the page to access and extract this node, you use the documentElement property.

Graphic

The code to access the root node is

var document_root = xmlData.documentElement;

Code

```
function join_fee(xmlData)
{
    var document_root = xmlData.documentElement;
}
```

The web page next needs to traverse the membership and join nodes. So you add the node properties that enable the page to access and extract these nodes.

Graphic

The required code is

var membership_node = document_root.firstChild;
var join_node = membership_node.lastChild;

Code

```
function join_fee(xmlData)
{
    var document_root = xmlData.documentElement;
    var membership_node = document_root.firstChild;
```

```
    var join_node = membership_node.lastChild;
}
```

You then configure the web page to extract the text nodes that store the joining fees.

Graphic

The code to access the node that stores the joining fee value is

var join_text = join_node.firstChild;

Code

```
function join_fee(xmlData)
{
    var document_root = xmlData.documentElement;
    var membership_node = document_root.firstChild;
    var join_node = membership_node.lastChild;
    var join_text = join_node.firstChild;
}
```

Finally, you use the nodeValue property to extract each joining fee value. You also add an alert message that can display this value. You can similarly step through other node hierarchies to extract values.

Graphic

The code to extract the joining fee value is

var join_amount = join_text.nodeValue;

Code

```
function join_fee(xmlData)
{
    var document_root = xmlData.documentElement;
    var membership_node = document_root.firstChild;
    var join_node = membership_node.lastChild;
    var join_text = join_node.firstChild;
    var join_amount = join_text.nodeValue;
    alert(join_amount+' to join this membership.');
}
```

But if you want to avoid stepping through hierarchies, you can also access a node directly by its tag name. To do this, you use the getElementsByTagName() method.

This method enables you to perform the following tasks:

- create an array of elements that have a specific tag name

- access each element in the array using a repeating loop, and

- access the siblings of each element

Suppose you want your web page to display the values stored in each set of name and month nodes and the associated attributes. So you first use the getElementsByTagName() method to create an array containing all the name elements.

Graphic

The code to do this is

var name_node = xmlData.getElementsByTagName('name');

Code

```
function findMembership(xmlData)
{
   // create an array of all elements named 'name'
   var name_node = xmlData.getElementsByTagName('name');
}
```

Next you pass on the name_node variable to a for loop. You also configure the loop to access each name element in the array and extract the value stored in the element.

Graphic

The following code accesses the current name element:

var name = name_node[i];

The following code extracts the value:

var name_value = name.firstChild.nodeValue;

Code

```
function findMembership(xmlData)
{
   // create an array of all elements named 'name'
   var name_node = xmlData.getElementsByTagName('name');

   // iterate through the array
   for (i=0; i<name_node.length; i++)
   {
      // get the name value from the name elements
      var name = name_node[i];
      var name_value = name.firstChild.nodeValue;
   }
}
```

In the loop, you then use the getElementsByTagName() method to create an array of month elements. And you add code to extract the value stored in each month element.

Graphic

The required code is

```
var month_node = xmlData.getElementsByTagName('month');
var month = month_node[i];
var month_value = month.firstChild.nodeValue;
```

Code

```
function findMembership(xmlData)
{
  // create an array of all elements named 'name'
  var name_node = xmlData.getElementsByTagName('name');

  // iterate through the array
  for (i=0; i<name_node.length; i++)
  {
    // get the name value from the name elements
    var name = name_node[i];
    var name_value = name.firstChild.nodeValue;

    // get the monthly fee from the month elements
    var month_node = xmlData.getElementsByTagName('month');
    var month = month_node[i];
    var month_value = month.firstChild.nodeValue;
  }
}
```

You now want to ensure that the value in the type attribute for a membership element is displayed next to the value in the corresponding name element. So you configure this code to extract the attribute values.

Code

```
// iterate through the array
for (i=0; i<name_node.length; i++)
{
  // get the name value from the name elements
  var name = name_node[i];
  var name_value = name.firstChild.nodeValue;

  // get the monthly fee from the month elements
  var month_node = xmlData.getElementsByTagName('month');
  var month = month_node[i];
  var month_value = month.firstChild.nodeValue;

  // get the optional 'type' attributes from the membership elements
  var mem_node = xmlData.                    ('membership');
  var mem_attr = mem_node[i].         ;
  var type_attr = mem_attr.              ('type');
```

```
            // append the type to the name if it was found

            {
                name_value += ' '+type_attr.nodeValue;
            }
        }
```

You use the getElementsByTagName() *method to create an array containing all the* membership elements.

Using the attributes *property, you access the attribute node for each* membership *element. You then pass on this node to the* mem_attr *variable.*

You configure the getNamedItem() *method to access the* type *attribute from each attribute node. You then store this attribute in the* type_attr *variable.*

With the if *statement, you first check for a value in the* type_attr *variable. If a value exists, the* if *statement extracts the value using the* nodeValue *property.*

Finally, you want to add the extracted XML data to your web page. To do this, you first use a div element to specify where the data should be added. You set the id value for this element to memberships, which is the root element for the rest of the XML data. You can use this value later to locate the div element.

Graphic

The code for the div element is

<div id="memberships"></div>

Code

```
        var mem_node = xmlData.getElementsByTagName('membership');
        var mem_attr = mem_node[i].attributes;
        var type_attr = mem_attr.getNamedItem('type');

        // append the type to the name if it was found
        if (type_attr)
        {
            name_value += ' '+type_attr.nodeValue;
        }
      }
    }

  </script>
  </head>
  <body>
```

```
    <h2>Membership Packages</h2>
    <form>
    <input type="button" value="Show Membership Options"
      onclick="loadXML();" />
    </form>
    <div id="memberships"></div>
  </body>
</html>
```

Next you create a paragraph element to act as a container within the div element for the extracted data. In addition, you create the variable, text, to store the data as a string.

Graphic

The code to create the paragraph element is

var paragraph = document.createElement('p');

The code for the text variable is

var text = name_value+' costs '+month_value+' per month';

Code

```
        var mem_node = xmlData.getElementsByTagName('membership');
        var mem_attr = mem_node[i].attributes;
        var type_attr = mem_attr.getNamedItem('type');

        // append the type to the name if it was found
        if (type_attr)
        {
           name_value += ' '+type_attr.nodeValue;
        }

        var paragraph = document.createElement('p');
        var text = name_value+' costs '+month_value+' per month';
      }
    }

  </script>
 </head>
 <body>
  <h2>Membership Packages</h2>
  <form>
  <input type="button" value="Show Membership Options"
    onclick="loadXML();" />
  </form>
  <div id="memberships"></div>
 </body>
</html>
```

You now need to add the text variable to the paragraph element. To do so, you first create a text node to enclose the text variable. Then you add this node to the paragraph element.

79

Graphic

The code to create the text node is

var text_node = document.createTextNode(text);

And the code to add the node to the paragraph element is
paragraph.appendChild(text_node);

Code

```
        var type_attr = mem_attr.getNamedItem('type');

        // append the type to the name if it was found
        if (type_attr)
        {
            name_value += ' '+type_attr.nodeValue;
        }

        var paragraph = document.createElement('p');
        var text = name_value+' costs '+month_value+' per month';
        var text_node = document.createTextNode(text);
        paragraph.appendChild(text_node);
      }
    }

  </script>
 </head>
 <body>
  <h2>Membership Packages</h2>
  <form>
  <input type="button" value="Show Membership Options"
   onclick="loadXML();" />
  </form>
  <div id="memberships"></div>
 </body>
</html>
```

To conclude the process, you add the paragraph element as a child node of the div element. You locate this div element by its id value, memberships. The getElementById() method facilitates this task.

Graphic

The code to locate the <div> element and add the paragraph element to it is

var membership_info = document.getElementById('memberships');
*   membership_info.appendChild(paragraph);*

Code

```
        // append the type to the name if it was found
        if (type_attr)
```

```
        {
          name_value += ' '+type_attr.nodeValue;
        }

        var paragraph = document.createElement('p');
        var text = name_value+' costs '+month_value+' per month';
        var text_node = document.createTextNode(text);
        paragraph.appendChild(text_node);
        var membership_info = document.getElementById('memberships');
        membership_info.appendChild(paragraph);
      }
    }

  </script>
  </head>
  <body>
    <h2>Membership Packages</h2>
    <form>
    <input type="button" value="Show Membership Options" onclick="loadXML();" />
    </form>
    <div id="memberships"></div>
  </body>
</html>
```

The XML data is finally added to the <div> element of the web page. You can now use *cascading style sheets*, or CSS, to display this data in the desired format.

Code

```
        // append the type to the name if it was found
        if (type_attr)
        {
          name_value += ' '+type_attr.nodeValue;
        }

        var paragraph = document.createElement('p');
        var text = name_value+' costs '+month_value+' per month';
        var text_node = document.createTextNode(text);
        paragraph.appendChild(text_node);
        var membership_info = document.getElementById('memberships');
        membership_info.appendChild(paragraph);
      }
    }

  </script>
  </head>
  <body>
    <h2>Membership Packages</h2>
    <form>
    <input type="button" value="Show Membership Options" onclick="loadXML();" />
    </form>
    <div id="memberships"></div>
  </body>
</html>
```

81

Question

You want to extract customer names from the XML variable, xmlDetails. Each name node is a first child and is at the second level from the root node.

Which steps should you perform first?

Code
```
// create variable to extract and store root node
var all_details = xmlDetails.MISSING CODE;

// create variable to extract and store first level node
var customer_node = all_details.firstChild;

// create variable to extract and store second level node
var name_node = customer_node.firstChild;

// create variable for the text node
var name_text = name_node.firstChild;

// extract value from text node
var name_val = name_text.MISSING CODE;
```

Options:

1. Create a container for the names using the createElement property
2. Access the root node using the documentElement property
3. Extract the names using the nodeValue property
4. Extract the names using the attributes property

Answer

Option 1: This option is incorrect. You use the createElement *property when adding data to a web page, not when extracting data.*

Option 2: This option is correct. Before you can extract a value from an XML file, you need to access its root node using the documentElement *property.*

Option 3: This option is correct. To extract the value stored in an XML node, you use the nodeValue *property.*

Option 4: This option is incorrect. You use the attributes *property to access the attribute node of an XML element. You can apply this property only after accessing the desired element by its tag name.*

Correct answer(s):

2. Access the root node using the documentElement property
3. Extract the names using the nodeValue property

Question

You want to add data extracted from an XML file to your web page. You've already stored this data in a text variable and created a paragraph container for the variable. You've also used the root node, products, to identify where on the page the data should be added.

What should you do to ensure that the data is added to the web page?

Options:

1. Create a node to enclose the text variable
2. Access each extracted data element by its name
3. Add the paragraph element to the page by using the products node
4. Extract the value stored in each child node of the text variable

Answer

Option 1: This option is correct. To add the text variable to the paragraph container, you first enclose the variable in a text node. You use the createTextNode *property to create this text node.*

Option 2: This option is incorrect. Because all items have been extracted and stored in a text variable, you don't need to access them separately. You only need to append the text variable to the paragraph container and add the paragraph container to the page.

Option 3: This option is correct. You need to add the paragraph element to the specified div element on the page. You can use the products *node to identify this element.*

Option 4: This option is incorrect. You've already created a paragraph container for the text variable. This implies that the text variable contains a string, not XML nodes. You don't need to extract values from this string. You can directly display it.

Correct answer(s):

1. Create a node to enclose the text variable
3. Add the paragraph element to the page by using the products node

3. Applying CSS styles dynamically

An XML document is only a set of nested tags and their attributes and values. When you open an XML document, you can view the values and attributes as well as the tags that enclose them. If you want to view only the values, formatted according to your requirements, you need to apply a CSS style to the document.

You can save CSS styles in a separate CSS document and pass on a reference to this document in your XML document. Alternatively, you can apply the CSS styles dynamically to the XML content in your web page.

To create a CSS document, you list the tag names, also known as selectors, and the styles you want to apply to them. You enclose each style declaration within curly brackets.

Code

```
name, month, join {
   display: block;
   font-family: Tahoma, Arial, Helvetica, sans-serif;
   }

name {color: #006699;}

month, join {color: red;}
```

After specifying the selectors and styles in a CSS document, you save it with a .css extension. For example, to the CSS document for memberships.xml, you assign the name memberships.css.

Code

```
name, month, join {
   display: block;
   font-family: Tahoma, Arial, Helvetica, sans-serif;
   }

name {color: #006699;}

month, join {color: red;}
```

You then add a path to the CSS document in the XML document.

In the example, a path to memberships.css is added in the memberships.xml file.

Graphic

The following XML code provides the path to memberships.css:

<?xml-stylesheet type="text/css" href="memberships.css"?>

Code

```
<?xml version="1.0"?>
<?xml-stylesheet type="text/css" href="memberships.css"?>
<memberships>
<membership type="unlimited">
<name>Full</name>
<month>$105</month>
<join>$450</join>
</membership>
<membership type="off-peak">
<name>Full Off-Peak</name>
<month>$75</month>
<join>$300</join>
</membership>
<membership>
<name>Fitness Only</name>
<month>$60</month>
<join>$250</join>
```

```
</membership>
<membership>
<name>Family</name>
<month>$250</month>
<join>$1000</join>
</membership>
</memberships>
```

Question

You're creating a CSS document.

Add code that applies the color green to a tag named grade. When doing so, use the color name instead of the hexadecimal value.

Code
```
name, grade, year {
    display: block;
    font-family: Tahoma, Arial, Helvetica, sans-serif;
    }
```

INSERT THE MISSING CODE

Answer

In a CSS document, to assign a style to the grade tag, you first add the tag name. Next to this, in curly brackets, you place the style declaration in the format color: green;.

Correct answer(s):

1. grade {color: green;}

To apply CSS styles dynamically, you use two JavaScript properties:

style and

The style property allows you to replace all the CSS styles, excluding styles marked important, that are applicable to a given selection. The replaced CSS styles may have been defined in an external CSS document or in the head element of your web page. If the CSS property you want to change is hyphenated, you rewrite it using camel casing. For example, you would rewrite font-size as fontSize.

Suppose you want to apply the font-family Tahoma to the contents of a variable xmlPara. To do so, you use this code.
The code is

xmlPara.style.fontFamily = "Tahoma"

className

To change the CSS class applied to any XML element on your web page, you use the className property.

Suppose you want to change the CSS class for an element from superscript to embossed. If the id of this element is textLine, you can change its CSS class using this code.

The code is

document.getElementById("textLine").className="embossed";

You're configuring an educational portal for children. On one of the pages, you want to allow users to learn about formatting styles and colors by actually modifying the onscreen text and the text they specify via text boxes.

You've added the required onscreen text to the page. You've also defined a CSS class, paragraph, for this text.

Graphic

The definition for the paragraph CSS class is

```
.paragraph {
    font-size: 12pt;
    font-family: Verdana, Arial, Helvetica, sans-serif;
    }
```

The code to add the onscreen text is

```
<p id="format_text" name="format" class="paragraph">
  <span id="Format">Format</span> <span id="this">this</span>
  <span id="text">text</span>.</p>
```

Code

```
<html>
  <head>
    <title>CSS and Javascript Example</title>
    <script type="text/javascript" language="Javascript">

    </script>
    <style type="text/css">

    .paragraph {
      font-size: 12pt;
      font-family: Verdana, Arial, Helvetica, sans-serif;
      }

    </style>
  </head>
  <body>
  <p id="format_text" name="format" class="paragraph">
    <span id="Format">Format</span> <span id="this">this</span>
    <span id="text">text</span>.</p>
  <form>
  </form>
```

```
</body>
</html>
```

Next you add two text boxes and two buttons to the page. You associate the id value word with the Word text box and the id value color with the Color text box. You also associate the change_color() and change_class() functions with the onclick events of the **Change Color** and **Bold** buttons, respectively.

Graphic

The code for the two text boxes is

```
Word: <input type="text" name="word" id="word" /><br />
Color: <input type="text" name="color" id="color" /><br />
```

And the code for the two buttons is

```
<input type="button" value="Change Color" onclick="change_color();" /><br />
<input type="button" value="Bold" onclick="change_class("bold");" />
```

Code

```
<script type="text/javascript" language="Javascript">

</script>
<style type="text/css">

.paragraph {
    font-size: 12pt;
    font-family: Verdana, Arial, Helvetica, sans-serif;
    }

</style>
</head>
<body>
<p id="format_text" name="format" class="paragraph">
  <span id="Format">Format</span> <span id="this">this</span>
  <span id="text">text</span>.</p>
<form>
  Word: <input type="text" name="word" id="word" /><br />
  Color: <input type="text" name="color" id="color" /><br />
  <input type="button" value="Change Color" onclick="change_color();" />
  <br />
  <input type="button" value="Bold" onclick="change_class("bold");" />
</form>
</body>
</html>
```

You want the change_color() function to apply a color to the user-specified text by using the style property. You also want the change_class() function to apply a new CSS class to the onscreen text. You want to use the className property to ensure that this function can override the existing CSS class.

You're now configuring the change_color() function. First, you ensure that the function can extract the values entered in the Word and Color text boxes.

Graphic

The code that extracts the values entered in the two text boxes is

```
word = document.getElementById('word').value;
color = document.getElementById('color').value;
```

Code

```html
<html>
 <head>
  <title>CSS and Javascript Example</title>
  <script type="text/javascript" language="Javascript">

  function change_color()
  {
     word = document.getElementById('word').value;
     color = document.getElementById('color').value;

     if (word == " || color == ")
     {
        alert('You must enter both a color and a word.');
        return false;
     }
  }

  </script>
  <style type="text/css">

  .paragraph {
     font-size: 12pt;
     font-family: Verdana, Arial, Helvetica, sans-serif;
     }
```

Next you declare a variable, el. To do this, you pass on the value from the Word text box.

Graphic

The code for the el variable is

```
el = document.getElementById(word);
```

Code

```html
 <head>
  <title>CSS and Javascript Example</title>
  <script type="text/javascript" language="Javascript">

  function change_color()
  {
     word = document.getElementById('word').value;
     color = document.getElementById('color').value;
```

88

```
    if (word == '' || color == '')
    {
        alert('You must enter both a color and a word.');
        return false;
    }

    el = document.getElementById(word);
}

</script>
<style type="text/css">

.paragraph {
    font-size: 12pt;
    font-family: Verdana, Arial, Helvetica, sans-serif;
}
```

You then assign the value from the Color text box to the color property of the el variable. The style property ensures that the color corresponding to this value is applied to the user-specified text in the Word text box.

Graphic

The code is

el.style.color = color;

Code

```
<title>CSS and Javascript Example</title>
<script type="text/javascript" language="Javascript">

function change_color()
{
    word = document.getElementById('word').value;
    color = document.getElementById('color').value;

    if (word == '' || color == '')
    {
        alert('You must enter both a color and a word.');
        return false;
    }

    el = document.getElementById(word);
    if (el)
    {
        el.style.color = color;
        return true;
    } else
    {
        alert('That was not a valid word.');
        return false;
```

```
    }
  }
```

Before you configure the change_class() function, you set its bold parameter. To do this, you define a CSS class, bold, within the style tags.

Graphic

The definition for the bold CSS class is

```
.bold {
    font-weight: bold;
  }
```

Code

```
<style type="text/css">

.paragraph {
   font-size: 12pt;
   font-family: Verdana, Arial, Helvetica, sans-serif;
   }

.bold {
   font-weight: bold;
   }

</style>
</head>
<body>
<p id="format_text" name="format" class="paragraph">
  <span id="Format">Format</span> <span id="this">this</span>
  <span id="text">text</span>.</p>
<form>
  Word: <input type="text" name="word" id="word" /><br />
  Color: <input type="text" name="color" id="color" /><br />
  <input type="button" value="Change Color" onclick="change_color();" />
  <br />
  <input type="button" value="Bold" onclick="change_class("bold");" />
</form>
</body>
</html>
```

Then you configure the function to retrieve the id value of the paragraph element, p, that encloses the onscreen text. You also assign the value bold to the className property of p. This ensures that the change_class() function can apply the bold CSS class to the onscreen text.

Graphic

The code is

```
p = document.getElementById("format_text");
p.className = "bold";
```

Code

```
color = document.getElementById('color').value;

if (word == '' || color == '')
{
    alert('You must enter both a color and a word.');
    return false;
}

el = document.getElementById(word);
if (el)
{
    el.style.color = color;
    return true;
} else
{
    alert('That was not a valid word.');
    return false;
}
}

function change_class("bold")
{
    p = document.getElementById("format_text");
    p.className = "bold";
}
</script>
```

Question

You've configured a CSS document to apply the Arial font family to all the XML text on your web page. However, you now want to apply the font family Helvetica to the text in an element named newWord.

Which code should you use?

Code
INSERT THE MISSING CODE.fontFamily = "Helvetica";

Options:

1. newWord.style
2. newWord.className
3. newWord{font-family: Helvetica;}

Answer

Option 1: *This option is correct. You use the* style *property to override a CSS style.*

91

Option 2: *This option is incorrect. The* className *property only allows you to modify the CSS class for an element.*

Option 3: *This option is incorrect. You would make this type of declaration in a CSS document.*

Correct answer(s):

1. newWord.style

Summary

You can configure your Ajax-based web pages to asynchronously display XML data. This data is structured into a hierarchical set of elements and attributes, so it's easy to systematically extract and display the data. You can use JavaScript objects and methods, such as XMLHttpRequest, to extract the data and add it to a web page. Then, if you want to format the data in a specific manner, you can apply CSS styles.

Ajax Troubleshooting

Learning Objectives

After completing this topic, you should be able to

- *handle errors in JavaScript*
- *use DOM inspectors*
- *use Ajax troubleshooting tools*

1. Using code to handle JavaScript errors

Developers commonly use the following tools and techniques to identify and fix errors in Ajax-based pages:

- error-handling code and tools for JavaScript

- Document Object Model, or DOM, inspectors for examining the DOM of a page, and

- troubleshooting tools for Ajax transactions

When you experience errors in an Ajax-based web page, you should first look to debug the JavaScript code. This code is often the root cause of many web page errors.

You typically find two types of errors in the JavaScript code:

syntax errors and

Syntax errors occur when you mistype keywords and tags or incorrectly nest tags. You can detect these errors when the code is being interpreted.

exceptions

If your code is incomplete – for example, if you don't declare a variable or function before calling it – exceptions may occur. An exception can affect all or part of your web page. Also, you can detect an exception only after the code is interpreted and loaded.

To efficiently handle syntax errors and exceptions, you should identify the erroneous lines and segments in your code.

To do so, you can use one of the following elements:

- a try statement or

- the window object

If you think a code segment is error prone, you can enclose it in a try statement. If the segment does have an error, the try statement stops executing. It also creates an Error object to store details about the error. These details include the error type and the machine-generated error message.

Code

```
try {
// code segment that shouldn't run in case of
// errors
}
```

If you want to retrieve the information stored in the Error object, you can add a catch statement.

Code

```
try {
// code segment that shouldn't run in case of
// errors
}

catch (err) {
// code to extract and display error type
// and error message
}
```

If you want to be alerted when the try statement completes, regardless of whether or not a problem occurred, you can append a finally statement to it. You can also use the finally statement to enclose code that you want to run in all circumstances.

Code

```
try {
// code segment that shouldn't run in case of
// errors
}

catch (err) {
// code to extract and display error type
```

```
// and error message
}

finally {
// code or messages that run in all cases
}
```

You can identify code errors quickly only if the catch statement retrieves and displays the necessary information. So you need to configure this statement correctly.

Code

```
catch (err) {
    alert ('Message: ' + err.message + ' \nError Type: '
    + err.name);
}
```

err

The err instance represents the Error *object generated by the* try *statement.*

message

The Error *object saves error messages in its* message *property. These messages are generated when the code in the* try *statement causes an error.*

name

The name *property of the* Error *object specifies an error-type code. You can use this code to identify the reason for the error.*

Supplement

Selecting the link title opens the resource in a new browser window.

Job Aid

Access the job aid **Error-Type Codes** to learn about the different error-type codes the name property can specify.

Just as the try statement creates an Error object when it encounters an error, the window object creates an error event. In this event, the window object stores the related error message, the URL of the page that triggered the error, and the line number at which the error occurred.

To handle the error event and capture the information stored in it, you use an event handler named onerror.

Say you're configuring JavaScript code for a web page. You want to use the onerror event handler to catch any errors.

You start by declaring a function, errorHandler(), that can capture and display the error message, URL, and line number related to each error. To store these details, you declare three variables: msg, url, and line.

Graphic

The following code is for the errorHandler() function:

function errorHandler(msg, url, line)
* {*
* alert('Error Message: ' + msg + '\nURL: '*
* + url +'\nLine Number: ' + line);*
* }*

Code

```
<script type="text/javascript">
  function errorHandler(msg, url, line)
  {
  alert('Error Message: ' + msg + '\nURL: '
  + url +'\nLine Number: ' + line);
  }
</script>
</head>
<body>

</body>
</html>
```

The error message you've passed on to the errorHandler() function is generated by the browser. If an error occurs, the browser can still display this error message separately.

However, you only want the errorHandler() function to display the message. So you configure the code to prevent the browser error message from displaying.

Graphic

The following code ensures that the browser doesn't display the error message:

return true;

Code

```
<script type="text/javascript">
  function errorHandler(msg, url, line)
  {
  alert('Error Message: ' + msg + '\nURL: '
  + url +'\nLine Number: ' + line);
  return true;
  }
</script>
</head>
<body>

</body>
</html>
```

You also declare the errorHandler() function as an onerror event handler, so that it can handle the error event.

Graphic

The code to declare the function as an onerror event handler is

onerror = errorHandler;

Code

```html
<script type="text/javascript">
  function errorHandler(msg, url, line)
  {
  alert('Error Message: ' + msg + '\nURL: '
  + url +'\nLine Number: ' + line);
  return true;
  }
</script>
</head>
<body>
<script type="text/javascript">
  onerror = errorHandler;
  //code
 </script>
</body>
</html>
```

If an error occurs now, the errorHandler() function can display the relevant error details.

Code

```html
<script type="text/javascript">
  function errorHandler(msg, url, line)
  {
  alert('Error Message: ' + msg + '\nURL: '
  + url +'\nLine Number: ' + line);
  return true;
  }
</script>
</head>
<body>
<script type="text/javascript">
  onerror = errorHandler;
  //code
 </script>
</body>
</html>
```

Question

You're creating JavaScript code for a web page. You want the dispError function to capture and display error details generated by a browser.

Which keyword should you include in the code?

Code

```
<script type="text/javascript">
  function dispError(msg, url, line)
  {
  alert('Error Message: ' + msg + '\nURL: ' + url +'\nLine Number: ' +
line);
  return true;
  }
</script>
</head>
<body>
<script type="text/javascript">
  INSERT THE MISSING CODE = dispError;
  //code
</script>
</body>
</html>
```

Options:

1. onerror
2. error
3. URIError

Answer

Option 1: *This option is correct. You use the* onerror *event handler to display error messages, the URL of the page that triggered the error, and the line number at which the error occurred.*

Option 2: *This option is incorrect. A browser generates an* error *event when a JavaScript error occurs, but you can't add this event directly to the code.*

Option 3: *This option is incorrect. The* URIError *keyword refers to an error type. Information about error types is stored in the* name *property of the* Error *object.*

Correct answer(s):

1. onerror

2. Tools for handling JavaScript errors

The checks you add to your JavaScript code may not catch all the errors. However, you can still identify missed errors in the code using add-ons and tools available in browsers.

One such error-checking tool is the Mozilla Error Console. After you open your web page in Firefox, you can access this tool from the **Tools** menu.

Graphic

You select the Error Console option on the Tools menu. Alternatively, you can press Ctrl+Shift+J. There are also other options on the Tools menu, such as Web Search, Downloads, Add-ons, Java Console, Firebug, DOM Inspector, Page Info, and Options.

When the Error Console first opens, the **All** button on the toolbar is selected by default. And the Console displays a list of all the JavaScript errors, warnings, and messages generated during the current browser session. The displayed list also includes errors and messages generated by the browser's menus, buttons, and border – the browser's *chrome*.

Graphic

The Error Console toolbar contains the buttons All, Errors, Warnings, Messages, and Clear. A text box named Code follows the toolbar. An Evaluate button appears next to the text box.

The Error Console dialog box also displays a list containing two items. Each item consists of a heading and a link to the file containing the erroneous code. A line of code is also included in the first item, and a line number appears next to each list item.

You can view a specific type of error by clicking the **Errors**, **Warnings**, or **Messages** buttons. You click the **Clear** button to clear the errors so that they're not cached and displayed the next time you access the Console.

You can also use the Console to identify errors in code that don't even belong to the current page. To do this, you type the external code in the Code box and click **Evaluate**.

Although the Error Console is useful for finding errors, it doesn't allow active debugging. If you want to debug your JavaScript code in Firefox, you can download and install the Firebug add-on and access it from the **Tools** menu.

Graphic

In the Tools menu, you select Firebug - Open Firebug. The Firebug submenu includes options such as Open Firebug, Open Firebug in New Window, Open With Editor, Text Size, Options, Firebug Online, Inspect Element, and Profile JavaScript.

After you launch Firebug, you can use two tabs to debug Ajax applications and pages.

Console

All errors that Firebug identifies during debugging are summarized on the Console tabbed page. Each summary list on this page has two lines. The first line specifies the error type, and the second line contains a snippet and line number of the erroneous code. Clicking an error's snippet opens the source code and highlights that particular error.

Script

You use the Script tabbed page to interactively debug the code in the current web page. This tabbed page displays the entire code, with the line containing the first error highlighted. Also, information about the error appears in a callout.

The Script tabbed page can either stop debugging when the next error occurs or continue debugging. You can use the **Break On Next** button to toggle between these two states. When the debugging stops, you can use the **Continue**, **Step Into**, **Step Over**, and **Step Out** buttons to step through the remaining code.

The Script tabbed page is divided into two panes. The first pane displays code from the current web page. This pane also contains a status bar. Five buttons and two drop-down lists appear on this status bar. The first button on the status bar is named Break On Next. The other buttons are Continue, Step Into, Step Over, and Step Out. The first drop-down list on the status bar displays the text all and the second drop-down list displays a filename. The second pane contains three tabs named Watch, Stack, and Breakpoints. The Watch tabbed page is open and displays only a box labeled New watch expression.

As you step through the code in the **Script** tab, you can set breakpoints at specific lines of code. When you next load your page, the debugging process pauses at these breakpoints.

To add a breakpoint to a line of code, you click the line number. A red dot then appears next to the line. You can remove the breakpoint by clicking this red dot.

You can also add conditions to a breakpoint. Doing so ensures that the debugging stops only when the breakpoint condition is met.

To add a condition to a breakpoint, you right-click the red dot that represents the breakpoint. Then you type the condition in the text box that appears.

Graphic

The text box that appears is named This breakpoint will stop only if this expression is true.

In Internet Explorer 8, you can use the Developer Tools utility to debug Ajax applications and pages.

Graphic

To access Developer Tools, you select Tools - Developer Tools from the Internet Explorer Command Bar. Alternatively, you can press F12. In addition to Developer Tools, the Tools menu displays other options such as Reopen Last Browsing Session, Pop-up Blocker, Manage Add-ons, Work Offline, Compatibility View Settings, Full Screen, Toolbars, Explorer Bars, and Suggested Sites.

After you launch Developer Tools, you can access the **Script** tab to debug the page currently open.

Graphic

The Developer Tools panel contains a menu bar and two panes. Options such as File, Find, Disable, View, Outline, Cache, and Tools appear on the menu bar.

The first pane consists of four tabs – HTML, CSS, Script, and Profiler. The HTML tabbed page is open to display a set of icons and HTML code. The second pane contains the buttons Style, Trace Styles, Layout, and Attributes.

The **Script** tab provides various buttons to enable you to debug an Ajax application or page.

As in Firebug, you can add breakpoints and conditional breakpoints to the code in the left pane. You can also use the debugging capabilities of Visual Studio with the Developer Tools utility, if required.

Graphic

The Script tabbed page is divided into two panes. The status bar for the first pane lists icons such as Continue, Break All, Break On Error, and Step Into. You can use these icons to step through the code.

This part of the status bar also includes the button Start Debugging, which you click to start debugging code. Next to this button is a drop-down list that allows you to select the web page file you want to debug.

The status bar for the second pane displays tabs named Console, Breakpoints, Locals, Watch, and Call Stack.

The Opera browser also includes a built-in debugging tool, Opera Dragonfly. You can access this tool from the browser's **Tools** menu.

Graphic

To access Dragonfly in Opera, you select Tools - Advanced - Opera Dragonfly. The Opera Tools menu displays options such as Mail and Chat Accounts, Delete Private Data, History, Downloads, Opera Unite, Notes, Links, and Advanced. The Advanced option is selected. The corresponding submenu displays options such as Cookies, Password Manager, Blocked Content, Plug-Ins, Cache, Opera Dragonfly, and Error Console.

In Dragonfly, you use the **Scripts** tab to debug the current web page.

Graphic

The Opera Dragonfly window contains the tabs DOM, Scripts, Network, Storage, Error Console, Utilities, and Settings.

The **Scripts** tab is divided into four sections.

Source

The Source section provides various buttons that enable you to scan for errors, step through the code, and add code breakpoints.
This section provides the following information:
Click the reload button above to fetch the scripts for the selected window.

Call Stack

The Call Stack section lists the functions and properties that caused the current error.

Command Line

You can type independent blocks of code in the Command Line section.

Inspection

In the Inspection section, you can view and inspect specific keywords and properties from the code displayed in the Source section.

Question

You want to use the Firefox Error Console to test your web page.

Identify the reasons why you would use this Console.

Options:

1. Allows you to selectively view errors, warnings, and messages
2. Allows you to add breakpoints to the code you're testing
3. Enables you to view the source code
4. Enables you to edit the source code

Answer

Option 1: *This option is correct. The Error Console dialog box contains three buttons:* **Errors***,* **Warnings***, and* **Messages***. These buttons let you view a list of errors, warnings, and messages, respectively.*

Option 2: *This option is incorrect. You can't debug the code using the Error Console, so you can't add code breakpoints.*

Option 3: *This option is correct. Each listing in the Error Console contains a hyperlink. You can click this hyperlink to view the source code in a new window.*

Option 4: *This option is incorrect. The Error Console only allows you to identify the errors in the code. It doesn't provide editing capabilities.*

Correct answer(s):

1. Allows you to selectively view errors, warnings, and messages
3. Enables you to view the source code

3. Using DOM inspectors

A DOM inspector allows you to view the DOM hierarchy of a web page and inspect each DOM element.

Three popular DOM inspectors are

- the Firefox DOM Inspector
- the DOM inspector in the Internet Explorer Developer Tools utility, and
- the Mouseover DOM Inspector, commonly known as MODI

The Firefox DOM Inspector is available as an add-on to Firefox. You can access it from the **Tools** menu.

Graphic

To do this, you select Tools - DOM Inspector. Alternatively, you can press Ctrl+Shift+I.

The Firefox DOM Inspector opens in a separate window and displays details about the current web page.

You can use its two panes to examine the DOM of the page.

Graphic

The DOM Inspector window displays a status bar and two panes. The status bar contains two buttons, a text box that displays the location of the currently loaded page, and a button named Inspect. The two panes, Document - DOM Nodes and Object - DOM Node follow the status bar.

Document - DOM Nodes

The Document - DOM Nodes pane displays the entire DOM of the page in a hierarchical structure. This structure is listed under a column named nodeName. You can manually browse through the structure and view the details of each element. You can also search for specific elements by their ids or tags, or by their attributes and attribute values.

The Document - DOM Nodes pane contains three sections: nodeName, id, and class. The nodeName section displays a hierarchical list of nodes. A node named TABLE, which is nested under another node named BODY, is selected.

Object - DOM Node

When you click an element in the Document - DOM Nodes pane, the element's details appear in the Object - DOM Node pane.

For example, when you click a tag, the Object - DOM Node pane displays the tag's local name, namespace URI, and node type. In addition, the pane displays the nodeName and nodeValue properties of each of the tag's attributes in a tabular format.

The Object - DOM Node pane contains two sections: nodeName and nodeValue. The nodeName section lists five attributes: cellspacing, cellpadding, border, align, and width. The nodeValue section lists the value of each of these attributes.

Say you want to search for a table element in the Document - DOM Nodes pane. You remember assigning the value 700 to the element's width attribute. To use these settings to search for the element, you click the **Find a node to inspect by id, tag, or attribute** button on the DOM Inspector toolbar.

Next, in the Find Nodes dialog box that opens, you select the **Attr** radio button. You type width in the Attr text box and 700 in the Value text box. Then you click **Find**.

Graphic

The Find Nodes dialog box contains two text boxes, Attr and Value, and two buttons, Find and Cancel. The dialog box also displays three radio buttons named Id, Tag, and Attr. The Attr radio button is selected.

Another **TABLE** node is then selected in the Document - DOM Nodes pane. This node corresponds to the table element in the code.

Graphic

The Object - DOM Node pane now lists the attributes for the selected TABLE node. The value of the width attribute is 700.

The DOM Inspector also enables you to select elements on the current web page and simultaneously view the corresponding nodes. To do this, you first click the **Inspect** button.

Next you click the **Find a node to inspect by clicking on it** button.

You can now click an element – for example, an image – on the docked page to view its corresponding node in the DOM Inspector.

The Developer Tools utility of Internet Explorer 8 also provides a built-in DOM inspector. You can access all the features of this inspector from the HTML tabbed page.

This tabbed page is divided into two panes. The first pane presents the DOM structure of the page open in the main Internet Explorer window. When you select an element in this pane, related information appears in the second pane.

Graphic

The Developer Tools panel is pinned to Internet Explorer. The HTML tabbed page is open in the panel.

In the first pane, you can click the **Edit** button to display and edit the source code. You can also immediately observe the effects of these edits, and any other edits you make via the HTML tabbed page, on the web page.

The first pane also offers a **Select Element by Click** button. If you want to identify the DOM node of an element on the web page, you first click this button and then the element. The corresponding DOM node is highlighted in the first pane, and information about the node appears in the second pane.

For example, to display the node for the gym room image, you click the **Select Element by Click** button and then click the image.

The information in the second pane is organized into four tabs.

Style

The Style tabbed page presents a tree view of the CSS classes applied to the selected element. The properties of each class are nested below it.
Each class has a checkbox next to it. In this example, every checkbox is selected.

Trace Styles

On the Trace Styles tabbed page, all the properties of the selected element appear in a tree view. The CSS class for a property is nested below it.
Each property has a checkbox next to it. In this example, every checkbox is selected.

Layout

The Layout tabbed page specifies the offset value, margin, border, padding, width, and height for the selected element.

Attributes

On the Attributes tabbed page, a two-column table presents the selected element's attributes and their values. You can edit an attribute or its value by double-clicking it. You can also add a new attribute, or delete an existing one, using the buttons available on this tabbed page.

If you want to use a DOM Inspector that is compatible with most modern browsers and consumes minimal system resources, you could choose the MODI DOM Inspector. This is a JavaScript-based favelet that you can add to and access from your browser's Bookmarks or Favorites folder.

The favelet is available at this MODI help page.

Graphic

The address of the MODI help page is http://slayeroffice.com/tools/modi/v2.0/modi_help.html.

The following information on the page is visible:
The Mouseover DOM Inspector, or MODI for short, is a favelet (also known as a bookmarklet) that allows you to view and manipulate the DOM of a web page simply by mousing around the document. Browsers currently supported are Firefox, Mozilla, Netscape 8, Opera 7.5+ and MSIE6+ on all of their respective Operating Systems. To begin using the Mouseover DOM Inspector, simply add the following link to your bookmarks by right clicking and selecting "Add to Favorites" or "Bookmark this Link" or whatever the nomenclature of your browser of choice.

Bookmark this link for MODIv2

To bookmark the favelet, right-click the **Bookmark this link for MODIv2** link on the help page. Then, from the shortcut menu, select the option that allows you to bookmark the link.

Graphic

For example, in Firefox, you select Bookmark This Link from the shortcut menu.

To inspect the DOM of a web page using MODI, browse to the web page and activate the MODI favelet from the browser's bookmark menu.

Graphic

For example, in Firefox, you select Bookmarks - Bookmark this link for MODIv2 to activate the favelet.

When activated, the MODI favelet appears as a pop-up window.

As you mouse over each element on the web page, the element's tag, attributes, dimensions, parent structures, and children appear in the pop-up window.

To regulate information presented by the MODI favelet, you can use various keyboard commands, such as

A

To copy the contents of the current element, press **A**. To then add the contents to another element, mouse over the element and press **S**.

W

Press **W** to access the DOM details of the current element's parent.

T, and

If you want to step through the DOM of the web page in a hierarchical, top-to-bottom manner, press **T**.

P

Press **P** to toggle between pausing and resuming the inspection process.

SkillCheck

You're examining the DOM of a web page using the Firefox DOM Inspector. Search for a div element whose id attribute has the value sprytooltip3.

Task:

1. Access the dialog box that allows you to find the div element by using the specified values.
2. Make sure that you can type the specified values in the dialog box.
3. Type in the specified values, and ensure that the related element can be searched.

Answer

To complete the task

*Step 1: Click the **Find a node to inspect by id, tag, or attribute** button*

*Step 2: Click the **Attr** radio button on the Find Nodes dialog box*

*Step 3: Type id in the Attr text box, sprytooltip3 in the Value text box, and then click **Find***

4. Troubleshooting Ajax transactions

Your Ajax-based web applications may malfunction if they cannot correctly exchange HTTP requests and responses with web browsers. However, Ajax applications don't support the mechanism that displays error messages when an HTTP transaction fails. If you want to detect these transaction errors, you need to use specialized troubleshooting tools, such as

- the Firebug add-on

- the Live HTTP headers extension for Firefox, and

- the ieHTTPHeaders Explorer Bar for Internet Explorer

In Firebug, the **Net** tab allows you to view all of the HTTP request headers your web pages send to a web server and the responses they receive.

Suppose you want to use Firebug to verify the HTTP transactions generated by a web site you've just configured. You've already browsed to the home page, launched the Firebug panel, and opened the Net tabbed page.

Graphic

On the toolbar of the Net tabbed page, the All tab is selected. Tabs named Clear, Persist, HTML, CSS, JS, XHR, Images, and Flash also appear on the toolbar.

The All tabbed page contains a five-column table, with URL, Status, Domain, Size, and Timeline as the column headings.

A node named GET parking.php4 appears under the URL column. Its status is 200 OK. Its domain, size, and timeline are also listed.

You click the **GET parking.php4** node to examine the first HTTP request sent by your browser to the web site.

Graphic

Five tabs – Params, Headers, Response, Cache, and HTML – now appear below the GET parking.php4 node. The Headers tabbed page is open.

The **Headers** tab contains two sections – Response Headers and Request Headers.

The Response Headers section lists details about the HTTP response.

In the Request Headers section, you can find details such as the host the request was sent to and the browser from which the request originated.

The Request Headers and Response Headers sections provide a detailed description of the HTTP requests and responses. However, you have to navigate through multiple tabs and buttons to access these details.

If you want a more compact presentation, where the requests and responses are listed on a single page, you should use the Live HTTP headers extension.

The Live HTTP headers extension is available as an add-on to Firefox. After you install the extension, you can launch it using the **Tools** menu.

Graphic

You select the Live HTTP headers option on the Tools menu.

Next you reload your web page. The ensuing HTTP transactions then appear on the Headers tabbed page of the Live HTTP headers dialog box.

Each HTTP request starts with the GET keyword and indicates the type of request that was sent. Other relevant details follow the GET statement.

Graphic

The Live HTTP headers dialog box contains four tabs – Headers, Generator, Config, and About. The Headers tabbed page is open and displays the HTTP requests and responses under the heading, HTTP Headers.

The dialog box also contains the buttons Save All, Replay, Clear, and Close. A checkbox named Capture appears next to the Replay button. The checkbox is selected, and the Save All, Replay, and Clear buttons are disabled.

The HTTP request on the Headers tabbed page is

GET /widgets/widget.php HTTP/1.1
Host: growsmartbusiness.com
User-Agent: Mozilla/5.O (Windows; U; Windows NT 6.1; en-GB; rv:1.9.2) Gecko/20100115 Firefox/3.6
Accept: text/html,application/xhtml+xml,application/xml;q=0.9,*/*;q=0.8
Accept-Language: en-gb,en;q=0.5
Accept-Encoding: gzip.deflate
Accept-Charset: ISO-8859-1,utf-8;q=O.7,*;q=0.7
Keep-Alive: 115
Connection: keep-alive

Referer: http://markup.widgetserver.com/syndication/get_widget.html?widget.appId=f2cf5a86-8b62-410f-aa0e-c2238aa3

To examine HTTP transaction details using Internet Explorer, you download and install another extension: the ieHTTPHeaders Explorer Bar.

Once installed, you can access this extension from the **Tools** menu.

Graphic

In the Tools menu, you select Explorer Bars – ieHTTPHeaders.

After opening the extension, you need to reload the web page. The extension then displays details of the HTTP transactions in the **Headers view** tab.

Graphic

The ieHTTPHeaders Explorer Bar extension is pinned to the current web page and displays two tabs – Headers view and Resource view. The Headers view tabbed page is open and displays HTTP requests and responses in separate paragraphs.

An excerpt from the content on the Headers view tabbed page is

GET/_media_/js/templates.php HTTP/1.1
Accept: */*
Referer: http://easynomadtravel.com/?xxxxx
Accept-Language: en-IN
User-Agent: Mozilla/4.O(compatible: MSIE8.0;

These details also appear in the **Resource view** tab, but in a tree-view format.

Graphic

In this tab, each main node in the tree view is a GET statement. The first GET statement in the tree view is expanded to display two subnodes.

SkillCheck

You've opened a web page in Internet Explorer. You now want to display a tree view of the HTTP transactions generated by this page.

To do so, access the tree view.

Task:

1. Access the tool that displays the tree view.
2. Ensure that the tree view is displayed.

Answer

To complete the task

*Step 1: Select **Tools - Explorer Bars - ieHTTPHeaders***

*Step 2: Click the **Resource view** tab*

Summary

Your Ajax-based web page may not function as desired if its JavaScript code contains errors. To identify and curtail these errors at the coding stage, you can use special coding techniques. For example, you can add try...catch statements and onerror event handlers to the code. You can also use browser add-ons, such as Firebug, to identify errors and debug them.

If you suspect that your web page's DOM has errors, you can use a DOM inspector, such as MODI, to identify these errors. In addition, you can use tools, such as the Live HTTP headers extension, to examine the HTTP requests and responses generated by the web page. You can then edit the page to fix any errors you identify in the DOM or in the HTTP transactions.

Using XML and Troubleshooting Tools in Ajax

Learning Objectives

After completing this topic, you should be able to

- *work with XML in Ajax applications*
- *use Ajax troubleshooting tools*

Exercise overview

In this exercise, you're required to display XML content in an Ajax-based web page. You're also required to identify and troubleshoot errors in Ajax applications.

This involves the following tasks:

- retrieving, formatting, and displaying XML content using JavaScript and CSS
- identifying errors in JavaScript code
- detecting errors in the DOM, and
- examining server requests and responses

Working with XML in Ajax

Case Study: Question 1 of 5

Scenario

For your convenience, the case study is repeated with each question.

You're creating an Ajax-based web site for a travel agency. Among other things, the web site will display details about major landmarks, tourist spots, and restaurants in a city. All these details are stored in XML files, which you've placed on a web server. You've also created CSS styles to apply a uniform look to each web page.

You now want to ensure that each web page can download and correctly display XML content from the XML files. You start by configuring settings for the restaurants.html page. You want this page to display restaurant details when the **Find Restaurants** button is clicked. You've saved the restaurant details in an XML file, restaurants.xml. In addition, you've associated the XML file with a CSS document, restaurants.css.

Refer to the learning aid **Current Code Status – Associated Files** to review the contents of the XML file and the CSS document. Then configure the restaurants.html page to display the restaurant details correctly.

To complete the required code, answer the following questions in order.

Question

You're adding a function, downloadContent(), to the restaurants.html page. You've already configured this function to download the restaurants.xml file.

What code should you now use to ensure that the contents of the downloaded file are stored in xmlDoc?

Code

```
var createObject = null;
function downloadContent()
{
    if (window.XMLHttpRequest)
    {
        createObject = new XMLHttpRequest();
    } else if (window.ActiveXObject)
    {
        createObject = new ActiveXObject("Microsoft.XMLHTTP");
    }
    if (createObject.overrideMimeType)
    {
        createObject.overrideMimeType("text/xml");
    }
    if (createObject)
    {
        createObject.open("GET", "restaurants.xml", true);
        createObject.onreadystatechange = function()
        {
            if (createObject.readyState == 4)
            {
                var xmlDoc = INSERT THE MISSING CODE
            }
        }
        createObject.send(null);
```

Answer

After download, the contents of the XML file are stored as a read-only object in the responseXML *property. So you pass this property to xmlDoc. When doing so, you employ the XMLHttpRequest instance,* createObject, *to which the property belongs.*

Correct answer(s):

1. createObject.responseXML;

Scenario

For your convenience, the case study is repeated with each question.

You're creating an Ajax-based web site for a travel agency. Among other things, the web site will display details about major landmarks, tourist spots, and restaurants in a city. All these details are stored in XML files, which you've placed on a web server. You've also created CSS styles to apply a uniform look to each web page.

You now want to ensure that each web page can download and correctly display XML content from the XML files. You start by configuring settings for the restaurants.html page. You want this page to display restaurant details when the **Find Restaurants** button is clicked. You've saved the restaurant details in an XML file, restaurants.xml. In addition, you've associated the XML file with a CSS document, restaurants.css.

Refer to the learning aid **Current Code Status – Associated Files** to review the contents of the XML file and the CSS document. Then configure the restaurants.html page to display the restaurant details correctly.

To complete the required code, answer the following questions in order.

Question

You next want to ensure that only the values – not the tags – stored in the restaurants.xml file are displayed. To do this, you first need to extract the values. You've already configured the code to extract the values from all the name elements.

Which code should you use to ensure that the values from the rating elements can be extracted?

Code
```
function findRestaurant(xmlDoc)
{
  var name_node = xmlDoc.MISSING CODE

  for (i=0; i<name_node.length; i++)
  {
    var name = name_node[i];
    var name_value = MISSING CODE

    var rating_node = xmlDoc.INSERT THE MISSING CODE;
    var rating = rating_node[i];
  }
}
```

Options:

1. getElementsByTagName('rating')
2. rating.firstChild.nodeValue
3. getNamedItem('rating')

110

Answer

Option 1: This option is correct. To extract the value stored in an XML element, you first need to access the element. The getElementsByTagName method enables you to access an element by its name.

Option 2: This option is incorrect. The nodeValue property allows you to extract the value stored in an element. However, you can use this property only after you access the element.

Option 3: This option is incorrect. You use the getNamedItem method to access an attribute's node by its name. In this case, rating is an element and not an attribute.

Correct answer(s):

1. getElementsByTagName('rating')

Case Study: Question 3 of 5

Scenario

For your convenience, the case study is repeated with each question.

You're creating an Ajax-based web site for a travel agency. Among other things, the web site will display details about major landmarks, tourist spots, and restaurants in a city. All these details are stored in XML files, which you've placed on a web server. You've also created CSS styles to apply a uniform look to each web page.

You now want to ensure that each web page can download and correctly display XML content from the XML files. You start by configuring settings for the restaurants.html page. You want this page to display restaurant details when the **Find Restaurants** button is clicked. You've saved the restaurant details in an XML file, restaurants.xml. In addition, you've associated the XML file with a CSS document, restaurants.css.

Refer to the learning aid **Current Code Status – Associated Files** to review the contents of the XML file and the CSS document. Then configure the restaurants.html page to display the restaurant details correctly.

To complete the required code, answer the following questions in order.

Question

You're now preparing to add the extracted data to the restaurants.html page. To do this, you first want to specify a DIV named restaurants to present the data.

Complete the code to do this in the restaurants.html page.

Code
```
<form>
<input type="button" value="Find Restaurants" onclick="downloadContent();" />
</form>
INSERT THE MISSING CODE
```

Answer

To specify a location for the extracted data, you use the div *element and give it the id* restaurants.

Correct answer(s):

1. <div id="restaurants"></div>

Case Study: Question 4 of 5

Scenario

For your convenience, the case study is repeated with each question.

You're creating an Ajax-based web site for a travel agency. Among other things, the web site will display details about major landmarks, tourist spots, and restaurants in a city. All these details are stored in XML files, which you've placed on a web server. You've also created CSS styles to apply a uniform look to each web page.

You now want to ensure that each web page can download and correctly display XML content from the XML files. You start by configuring settings for the restaurants.html page. You want this page to display restaurant details when the **Find Restaurants** button is clicked. You've saved the restaurant details in an XML file, restaurants.xml. In addition, you've associated the XML file with a CSS document, restaurants.css.

Refer to the learning aid **Current Code Status – Associated Files** to review the contents of the XML file and the CSS document. Then configure the restaurants.html page to display the restaurant details correctly.

To complete the required code, answer the following questions in order.

Question

Next you save the extracted data in a readable format in a variable named text. You also create a paragraph container for the extracted data.

What should you do to ensure that the contents of the text variable are added to the web page?

Code
```
function findRestaurant(xmlDoc)
{
  var name_node = xmlDoc.getElementsByTagName('name');

  for (i=0; i<name_node.length; i++)
  {
    var name = name_node[i];
    var name_value = name.firstChild.nodeValue;

    var rating_node = xmlDoc.getElementsByTagName('rating');
    var rating = rating_node[i];
    var rating_value = rating.firstChild.nodeValue;

    var cuisine_node = xmlDoc.getElementsByTagName('cuisine');
    var cuisine = cuisine_node[i];
    var cuisine_value = cuisine.firstChild.nodeValue;

    var paragraph = document.createElement('p');
    var text = name_value+' has a rating of '+rating_value+'
          and serves '+cuisine_value+' cuisine';
    var text_node = document.createTextNode(text);
```

```
            MISSING CODE;
            var restaurant_info = document.getElementById('restaurants');
            restaurant_info.appendChild(paragraph);
        }
    }
```

Options:

1. Create a node for the paragraph container
2. Add the paragraph container to the text variable
3. Add the text variable node to the paragraph container
4. Configure the text variable to be transferred directly to the div element

Answer

Option 1: *This option is incorrect. A paragraph container has already been created. You've also configured code that adds this container to the div element you'd specified earlier. You don't need to create another node for the paragraph container.*

Option 2: *This option is incorrect. The paragraph container is meant to hold the text variable. So you should add the text variable, by its node, to the paragraph container.*

Option 3: *This option is correct. You've already ensured that the paragraph container can be added to the web page. You should also add the text variable node to the paragraph container. This ensures that the data in the text variable can be added to and displayed at the specified location.*

Option 4: *This option is incorrect. Before you can transfer the text variable, you should add it to the paragraph container. You can then add the paragraph container to the location where you want to display the variable's contents.*

Correct answer(s):

3. Add the text variable node to the paragraph container

Case Study: Question 5 of 5

Scenario

For your convenience, the case study is repeated with each question.

You're creating an Ajax-based web site for a travel agency. Among other things, the web site will display details about major landmarks, tourist spots, and restaurants in a city. All these details are stored in XML files, which you've placed on a web server. You've also created CSS styles to apply a uniform look to each web page.

You now want to ensure that each web page can download and correctly display XML content from the XML files. You start by configuring settings for the restaurants.html page. You want this page to display restaurant details when the **Find Restaurants** button is clicked. You've saved the restaurant details in an XML file, restaurants.xml. In addition, you've associated the XML file with a CSS document, restaurants.css.

Refer to the learning aid **Current Code Status – Associated Files** to review the contents of the XML file and the CSS document. Then configure the restaurants.html page to display the restaurant details correctly.

To complete the required code, answer the following questions in order.

Question

Having added the desired text to the web page, you're now formatting specific sections of the text.

You want the names of the restaurants offering discounts to appear olive green. However, if a user selects one of these restaurants to book a table, you want the name of the restaurant to also appear bold. You've already added the required CSS classes to the page and ensured that the restaurant names appear olive green.

What should you do now to ensure that the names of the selected restaurants appear both olive green and bold?

Options:

1. Add the new styles to the CSS document linked to the restaurants.xml file
2. Configure the head element of the web page to use the new styles
3. Configure the style property to pass the correct CSS class to the selected names
4. Use the className property to apply the desired CSS class to the selected names

Answer

Option 1: *This option is incorrect. In a CSS document, you define styles for tags. You can't define styles for specific values stored in the tags.*

Option 2: *This option is incorrect. The styles in the* head *element apply to the entire web page. If you want to apply styles selectively to one or more sections of the web page, you should configure inline styles.*

Option 3: *This option is incorrect. The* style *property allows you to replace styles defined in an external CSS document or in the* head *element of your web page. You can't use it to modify the effect of inline CSS classes.*

Option 4: *This option is correct. You use the* className *property to change the CSS class applied to any XML element on a web page.*

Correct answer(s):

4. Use the className property to apply the desired CSS class to the selected names

Identifying errors in code

Question

You're creating JavaScript code for your web page. You want the code to alert you when an error occurs. The alert should specify the browser-generated error message, the URL of the page that triggered the error, and the line number that contains the error.

What should you do?

Options:

1. Add code that creates an error event

2. Add an instance of the onerror event handler
3. Configure an instance of the Error object
4. Use a catch statement to display the error details

Answer

Option 1: This option is incorrect. When an error occurs in JavaScript code, the browser automatically creates an error *event. This event contains the browser-generated error message and details about where the error occurred.*

Option 2: This option is correct. To retrieve and display the information stored in an error event, *you configure an instance of the* onerror *event handler.*

Option 3: This option is incorrect. An Error *object only stores details about the error type and the machine-generated error message. It doesn't specify the location where the error occurred.*

Option 4: This option is incorrect. A catch *statement retrieves the information stored in the* Error *object. This means that the* catch *statement can't specify where the error occurred.*

Correct answer(s):

2. Add an instance of the onerror event handler

Question

You want to view any browser-generated error messages regarding a block of code. You've already created a function, dispError, to display the error message.

Which line should you add immediately above the code?

Code
```
<script type="text/javascript">
  INSERT THE MISSING CODE
  //block of code
</script>
```

Answer

If a JavaScript error occurs, the browser creates an error *event. This event contains details about the error. To ensure that the* dispError *function can extract these error details, you should declare the function as an instance of the* onerror *event handler.*

Correct answer(s):

1. onerror = dispError;

Question

You're adding a function named errorHandle to your JavaScript code.

Make sure that the function can retrieve and display the error details generated by the window object.

115

Code

```
<script type="text/javascript">
   function INSERT THE MISSING CODE
   {
   alert('Error Message: ' + msg + '\nURL: ' + url +'\nLine Number: ' +
line);
   return true;
   }
</script>
</head>
<body>
```

Options:

1.   errorHandle(msg, url, line)
2.   err(message, name)
3.   window(onerror)

Answer

Option 1: This option is correct. You should ensure that errorHandle *can retrieve and display the browser-generated error message, the URL of the page that triggered the error, and the line number that contains the error.*

Option 2: This option is incorrect. The err *instance is not an event handler. It represents the* Error *object generated by the* try *statement.*

Option 3: This option is incorrect. You use the onerror *event handler to handle the* error *event generated by the* window *object. So you should configure* errorHandle *as an instance of* onerror. *However, before this, you must ensure that* errorHandle *can display relevant details –* msg, url, *and* line.

Correct answer(s):

1.   errorHandle(msg, url, line)

Detecting errors in the DOM

Your team is developing an Ajax-based web site for an educational portal, Imagenie. One of your team members has sent you the first few pages of the web site for review.

When browsing through the home page, you identify page elements that are configured and formatted incorrectly. For example, the **simple** button is misaligned.

To identify the reason for these errors, you decide to inspect the page's DOM using the Firefox DOM Inspector. You've already installed this add-on.

SkillCheck

You've opened the Imagenie home page in Firefox.

Now access the DOM Inspector. For easy inspection, ensure that the home page is docked with the Inspector window.

On the Imagenie home page, the simple button appears in the Properties section. This section is placed immediately below the Button Preview section.

Task:

1. First open the DOM Inspector window.
2. Ensure that the home page is nested below the DOM Inspector.

Answer

To complete the task

Step 1: *Select* **Tools - DOM Inspector**
Using keyboard: *The keyboard alternative is* **Ctrl+Shift+I**.

Step 2: *Click* **Inspect**

SkillCheck

You want to examine the style applied to the **simple** button. To do this, you first need to access the **simple** button's node.

Use the DOM Inspector toolbar and the Browser panel to quickly access the **simple** button's node. You've already browsed to the **simple** button in the Browser panel.

Task:

1. Ensure you can use the Browser panel to quickly access the **simple** button's node.
2. Identify the **simple** button as the item with the node you want to inspect.

Answer

To complete the task

Step 1: *Click the* **Find a node to inspect by clicking on it** *button on the DOM Inspector toolbar*

Step 2: *Click the* **simple** *button in the Browser panel*

Examining requests and responses

You're testing whether your web site can correctly interact with all types of browsers. To begin with, you decide to find out if Firefox can successfully send requests to and receive responses from the site.

Graphic

The address of the web site is

www.diallonic.com

You've already opened Firefox and have attempted to browse to the web site. You now want to view the HTTP requests and responses that are generated during this transaction.

SkillCheck

For easy and quick error identification, you want the HTTP requests and responses to be listed chronologically on a single page. You don't want a tabbed presentation or the details to be presented in a tree view.

Access the Firefox add-on that allows you to view details about each HTTP request and response pair, as it is generated, on a single page.

Task:

1. First open the add-on window.

Answer

To complete the task

Step 1: Select **Tools - Live HTTP headers**

XML content has been downloaded and displayed in the desired format in an Ajax-based web page. In addition, coding techniques and Ajax troubleshooting tools have been used to identify errors in web pages.

Ajax and Web Services

Learning Objectives

After completing this topic, you should be able to

- *recognize key characteristics of web services*
- *consume a web service in Ajax via an application proxy*
- *consume a web service in Ajax using the script tag hack*

1. Key characteristics of web services

For a simple, noncommercial Ajax-based web application, you can create downloadable XML content from scratch. However, this type of creation can prove expensive and time consuming if you want to add complex features and functions through the content.

For example, you might want to validate form data and offer secure logon access to users. You might also want to provide traffic alerts, news feeds, and other information based on a user's location. To create content for these, you'd have to learn complex server-side code, which can be difficult to master.

To avoid this extra effort, you can use *web services* and *application programming interfaces*, or APIs.

A web service contains all the code and XML content required to generate data, such as traffic alerts and weather updates. An organization that provides a web service usually places it on its web server. You only need to call this web service from your application to use its features.

An API is similar to a web service and allows you to display portions of a web site in your application. For example, you can use the Yahoo! Music API to display content from the Yahoo! Music catalog. And you can use a Google API to display a web-search feature or a section of Google Maps.

You can also combine multiple web services and APIs to create a hybrid service called a *mashup*. For example, you can create a mashup by combining the Google Maps API with a web service that provides weather updates. This mashup will allow you to determine the weather conditions at any location you select in the Google Maps API.

Many Ajax developers prefer to use web services because they consume minimal system resources, offer varied functionality, and work in the background. This last feature ensures that users can interact with other elements on an Ajax page while a web service processes requests.

Additionally, web services are compatible with available techniques for downloading and displaying data. If you can download and display content from a self-created XML document, you can also do the same with a web service.

Before you begin identifying web services for your application, you should consider their disadvantages.

Some of these disadvantages are

slow response time

A web service could slow down while your application extracts XML data from it. This can also slow down the entire application.

few sponsors, and

Although web services are useful, very few businesses sponsor their development. The lack of widespread knowledge about web services is the main reason for this. Because web services work in the background, most users aren't even aware of their existence. As a result, potential sponsors don't foresee any promotional value in sponsoring web-service development.

Lack of sponsorship can force a web-service developer to cease operations. So you should opt for a web service that has adequate financial backing.

high maintenance cost

All web services need to be constantly available, and so they are expensive to maintain and use. Their development costs are also considerable. These costs can translate into high selling prices.

However, most potential customers look for free or inexpensive third-party web services. That's why most web services are developed and maintained by large companies, which can afford to distribute them for free or at nominal rates.

You should look for web services that don't have the characteristic disadvantages. You can find many such services on the Internet. Most of them are free and are also backed by strong support groups.

The following are a few web sites that offer free, but efficient and lasting, web services:

- XMethods
  The address of the web site is

  http://www.xmethods.com/ve2/index.po

- Yahoo! Developer Network
  The address of the web site is

  http://www.developer.yahoo.com

- WEBSERVICES.ORG, and
  The address of the web site is

  http://www.webservices.org/

- webserviceX.NET
  The address of the web site is

  http://www.webservicex.net/WCF/default.aspx

If you gain access to suitable web services and incorporate them in your Ajax application, you can enhance the application's usability. This can also increase user traffic to the application and ultimately increase your profits.

Suppose your Ajax application caters to tourists. You want to incorporate a search feature that allows users to find out weather conditions anywhere in the United States.

A web service available at webserviceX.NET enables this type of feature. This web service is part of the Utilities category, under the Web Services Category section of the webserviceX.NET home page.

Graphic

The Web Services Category section of the webserviceX.NET home page displays links named Business and Commerce, Standards and Lookup Data, Other Web Services, Value Manipulation / Unit Convertor, Communications, Graphics and Multimedia, and Utilities.

To view details about the required web service, you click the **Global Weather** link in the Utilities category.

Graphic

The Utilities page displays links such as USA Weather Forecast, SunSetRiseService, GeoIPService, Translation Engine, and Global Weather. The Global Weather link is clicked.

On the Global Weather page, a summary of the web service's features and related URLs appears. The most important among these URLs is the endpoint. This endpoint URL allows you to view and use the methods available in the web service. All web service endpoints have an .asmx extension.

Graphic

The Global Weather page contains sections named Summary, Endpoint, Disco, WSDL Location, and Demo. The Endpoint, Disco, and WSDL Location sections display URLs.

The URL in the Endpoint section is

http://www.webservicex.net/globalweather.asmx

Before you integrate the Global Weather web service with your application, you should test the service and learn how it functions.

To test the service, you perform three steps:

access the web service's endpoint via a browser

To access the methods the web service offers, you browse to the endpoint of the service. This opens the endpoint page, which displays links to two methods.

The endpoint page for the GlobalWeather Web Service is open. The methods listed on this page are GetCitiesByCountry and GetWeather. The first method allows you to get all major cities by country name (full or part). The second method allows you to get weather reports for all major cities around the world.

click the link to the method you want to use, and

Because you want to determine the weather conditions in a US city, you click the **GetWeather** link.

invoke a weather search

On the GetWeather page, invoke a search for the current weather conditions in Chicago. To do this, you first type Chicago and United States in the CityName and CountryName text boxes, respectively. Then you click **Invoke**. This creates and sends a request header, which uses the HTTP POST method.

The GetWeather page contains a section named Test. This section contains two text boxes named CityName and CountryName and a button named Invoke.

The search result is in XML format and is enclosed within <string> tags.

To display relevant data from this result in your Ajax application, you first need to ensure that the application retrieves the result. Then you need to configure the application to parse the result and extract data from it.

To determine the type of code to configure, you should find out how a web application processes web-service requests and responses.

You can consider this processing a four-step transaction:

Graphic

The animation depicts an Ajax web page establishing an HTTP connection with a server that hosts a web service. Over this connection, the application sends a data request to the server. In response, the server sends back the required XML data. The application then processes and displays this data.

1. The application uses a protocol, such as HTTP, to connect to the web service.
2. The application sends a request to the server that hosts the web service.
3. The server sends back a response. This response could simply specify that the request was successfully received. Or, it could also include the data requested by the application.
4. The application processes the response and retrieves the relevant data. Then the application either closes the connection or sends other web-service requests.

In the webserviceX.NET example, the four-step transaction starts when you click the **Invoke** button. This establishes an HTTP connection with the service and sends the query strings to the service. The query strings are enclosed in the body of an HTTP POST request header. The HTTP GET method and SOAP can also be used to create the headers.

Graphic

The following is the code for the HTTP POST request header:

POST /globalweather.asmx/GetWeather HTTP/1.1
Host: webservicex.net
Content-Type: application/x-www-form-urlencoded
Content-Length: 40

CityName=Chicago&CountryName=United%20States

A standard request header that you send to a web service should contain details such as

- the web service name and the protocol used to establish a connection with the service

- the HTTP method being used

- the information that you want to process

- the length of the information

- the format in which the request should be sent

- details about the browser or application that initiated the request, and

- the date the request was initiated

It can be difficult to include all these details in an HTTP GET query or a simple POST header. That's why web standard consortiums recommend the use of SOAP to create request headers. SOAP allows you to create a separate document to store the header details.

SOAP also performs the following tasks:

- encrypts request headers to ensure security

- sorts and processes the headers based on priority and expiration dates, and

- keeps track of the headers as they travel from the client to the server

The example depicts a SOAP document that contains a request header for the Global Weather web service.

Code

```
POST /globalweather.asmx HTTP/1.1
Host: webservicex.net
Content-Type: text/xml; charset=utf-8
Content-Length: 40
SOAPAction: "http://www.webserviceX.NET/GetWeather"
```

```
<?xml version="1.0" encoding="utf-8"?>
                    xmlns:xsi="http://www.w3.org/2001/XMLSchema-instance"
xmlns:xsd="http://www.w3.org/2001/XMLSchema"
xmlns:soap="http://schemas.xmlsoap.org/soap/envelope/">

  <GetWeather xmlns="http://www.webserviceX.NET">
   <CityName>Chicago</CityName>
   <CountryName>United%20States</CountryName>
  </GetWeather>
```

<soap:Envelope> *is the parent tag that specifies the namespace to which the contents of the SOAP document should conform. It encloses the header and the body of the SOAP document. The header information is enclosed in* <SOAP:Header> *tags and can include user credentials. The* <SOAP:Header> *tags aren't part of the example.*

The standard request header details are enclosed in the <soap:Body> *tags. In the example, the tags enclose the web service name and the query strings you want to send to the service.*

In response to the SOAP request, the web service sends another SOAP document. The example depicts an excerpt from this document.

Code

```
HTTP/1.1 200 OK
Content-Type: text/xml; charset=utf-8
Content-Length: length

<?xml version="1.0" encoding="utf-8"?>
<soap:Envelope xmlns:xsi="http://www.w3.org/2001/XMLSchema-instance"
xmlns:xsd="http://www.w3.org/2001/XMLSchema"
xmlns:soap="http://schemas.xmlsoap.org/soap/envelope/">
 <soap:Body>
  <GetWeatherResponse xmlns="http://www.webserviceX.NET">
   <GetWeatherResult><CurrentWeather>
<Time>Apr 07, 2010 - 01:52 PM EDT / 2010.04.07 1752 UTC</Time>
<Wind> from the NNE (020 degrees) at 8 MPH (7 KT):0</Wind>
<Visibility> 8 mile(s):0</Visibility>
<SkyConditions> overcast</SkyConditions>
<Temperature> 45.0 F (7.2 C)</Temperature>
<DewPoint> 42.1 F (5.6 C)</DewPoint>
<RelativeHumidity> 89%</RelativeHumidity>
<Pressure> 29.69 in. Hg (1005 hPa)</Pressure>
<Status>Success</Status>
</CurrentWeather></GetWeatherResult>
  </GetWeatherResponse>
 </soap:Body>
</soap:Envelope>
```

To extract and display content from this response document, you need to apply both XML and SOAP standards. This can be a tedious and time-consuming task.

If you want to avoid the tedious coding process, you can use the Representational State Transfer, or REST, approach instead of SOAP.

The REST approach uses HTTP methods to send requests and receive responses. For example, to retrieve weather information from the Global Weather web service, you can send this URL-based query.

Code

```
http://webservicex.net/globalweather.asmx/
GetWeather?CountryName=United%20States&CityName=Chicago
```

The REST approach has several advantages:

Code

```
http://webservicex.net/globalweather.asmx/
GetWeather?CountryName=United%20States&CityName=Chicago
```

- uses simple HTTP methods such as GET and POST to send requests

- retrieves information only in XML format

- ensures the security of requests and responses by using authentication mechanisms, and

- sends requests via URLs, which are easy to authenticate

The REST approach isn't as secure as SOAP, however. One reason for this is that, unlike SOAP, REST doesn't keep track of a request while it travels between the client and the server. Also, you can't create lengthy queries when using the GET method to send REST requests.

If you ignore these disadvantages, you can safely use REST to exchange data with web services.

Code

```
http://webservicex.net/globalweather.asmx/
GetWeather?CountryName=United%20States&CityName=Chicago
```

Question

Match each approach to creating request and response headers with its characteristics. You can match each approach with more than one characteristic.

Options:

A.   SOAP

B. REST

Targets:

1. Imposes a limit on the length of queries, and retrieves information only in XML format
2. Sends a request within a document, and encrypts request headers
3. Keeps track of requests as they travel between the client and the server
4. Processes request headers based on priority
5. Allows easy authentication of requests

Answer

If you use the GET method in REST requests, you can't create lengthy queries. And the response you receive to a REST request is in XML format.

The SOAP approach creates a separate SOAP document for each request header. This approach also allows you to encrypt the request headers.

SOAP keeps track of a request even when it's traveling between the client and the server. This makes SOAP more secure than REST.

SOAP sorts and processes request headers based on their priority and expiration dates.

REST requests sent via URLs are easy to authenticate.

Correct answer(s):

Target 1 = Option B

Target 2 = Option A

Target 3 = Option A

Target 4 = Option A

Target 5 = Option B

2. Using a proxy to consume a web service

If a web service is located in the same domain as your application, you can consume the web service using the XMLHttpRequest object. In this case, you can pass on the endpoint of the service to the open() method and extract data from the service.

The example depicts how you can pass on an endpoint named globalweather.asmx, which is in the same domain as your application.

Graphic

The code that passes on the endpoint to the open() method is

ajaxObject.open("GET", "globalweather.asmx", true);

Code

```
    ajaxObject = new XMLHttpRequest();
  } else if (window.ActiveXObject)
  {
    ajaxObject = new ActiveXObject("Microsoft.XMLHTTP");
  }
  if (ajaxObject.overrideMimeType)
  {
    ajaxObject.overrideMimeType("text/xml");
  }
  if (ajaxObject)
  {
    ajaxObject.open("GET", "globalweather.asmx", true);
    ajaxObject.onreadystatechange = displayXML;
    ajaxObject.send(null);
  }
```

Problems occur when a web service is located in a different domain. These problems are triggered by users' browser settings.

For example, in Firefox, your application stops responding as soon as the open() method is called. Firefox is configured to block applications that attempt to access services stored on a different domain.

Graphic

The code to pass on a web service that is located in a different domain is

var endpoint = "http://webservicex.net/globalweather.asmx";
*   ajaxObject.open("GET", endpoint, true);*

Code

```
    ajaxObject = new XMLHttpRequest();
  } else if (window.ActiveXObject)
  {
    ajaxObject = new ActiveXObject("Microsoft.XMLHTTP");
  }
  if (ajaxObject.overrideMimeType)
  {
    ajaxObject.overrideMimeType("text/xml");
  }
  if (ajaxObject)
  {
    var endpoint = "http://webservicex.net/globalweather.asmx";
    ajaxObject.open("GET", endpoint, true);
    ajaxObject.onreadystatechange = displayXML;
    ajaxObject.send(null);
  }
```

In Internet Explorer, access to the web service depends on the browser settings for the cross-domain access.

For example, if the **Disable** radio button is selected, your application can't access the web service. And if the **Prompt** radio button is selected, Internet Explorer asks for the user's permission to allow access to the service.

Graphic

The Security Settings – Internet Zone page of the Internet Options dialog box is open. On this page, under Settings, the Miscellaneous section is selected. And its Access data sources across domains subsection is highlighted. This subsection contains three radio buttons named Disable, Enable, and Prompt. The Disable radio button is selected.

Note

*To open the Security Settings – Internet Zone page, in the Internet Options dialog box, first click the **Security** tab and then click the **Custom level** button.*

The browsers' response to the open() method call is the result of a proactive security check – *same origin security policy*. This check ensures that a web application doesn't inadvertently transfer viruses to other servers via an external web service.

Code

```
  ajaxObject = new XMLHttpRequest();
} else if (window.ActiveXObject)
{
  ajaxObject = new ActiveXObject("Microsoft.XMLHTTP");
}
if (ajaxObject.overrideMimeType)
{
  ajaxObject.overrideMimeType("text/xml");
}
if (ajaxObject)
{
  var endpoint = "http://webservicex.net/globalweather.asmx";
  ajaxObject.open("GET", endpoint, true);
  ajaxObject.onreadystatechange = displayXML;
  ajaxObject.send(null);
}
```

You can't change the same origin security policy. However, you can add hacks or temporary solutions to your Ajax applications so that they bypass the policy checks.

The hacks you can use to bypass the same origin security policy include

- application proxies

- <script> tag hacks, and

- newer alternatives such as FlashXMLHttpRequest, ContextAgnosticXMLHttpRequest, and JSONRequest

When using the application proxy hack, you create an additional chunk of code, or *proxy*, and save it on your web server.

Next you configure the XMLHttpRequest object to call the proxy. The proxy interacts with the web server on the object's behalf and returns the required response.

You can use either ASP.NET or PHP to create a proxy.

The example depicts the ASP.NET code you can use to create a proxy.

Code

```
<%@Page Language = "C#" Debug="true" %>
<%@ import Namespace="System.xml" %>
<script language="C#" runat="Server" %>

 void Page_Load()
 {
                         = new XmlDocument();
             = "http://webservicex.net/globalweather.asmx/
    GetWeather?CountryName=United%20States&CityName="
     + Request.QueryString["city"].ToString();
                   ;
  string xml =                  ;
  Response.ContentType = "text/xml";
  Response.Write(xml);
 }
</script>
```

You declare Dom *as an instance of the* XmlDocument *object. This object provides methods to access and extract XML data from the web service.*

In a string variable named url, *you store the REST query you want to send to the web service. In this query, you assign a fixed value to the* CountryName *variable. That's because you want your application to provide weather details only for US cities.*

You use the Load *method of the* XmlDocument *object to pass on the value stored in the* url *variable to the* Dom *variable.*

Using the InnerXml *property, you assign the retrieved value to a string named* xml. *You also configure this value to be written to the response stream.*

You decide to use a PHP proxy, though, because it has more compact code.

In the proxy, you first pass on your query to the URL variable.

Graphic

128

The code to declare the URL variable is

$URL = 'http://webservicex.net/globalweather.asmx/
GetWeather?CountryName=United%20States&CityName=';

Code

```php
<?php
header('Content-Type: text/xml');

$URL = 'http://webservicex.net/globalweather.asmx/
   GetWeather?CountryName=United%20States&CityName=';
?>
```

Then you use the DOMDocument method to store the value retrieved by the query in the xml variable.

Graphic

To do this, you use the following code:

$xml = DOMDocument::load($URL);

Code

```php
<?php
header('Content-Type: text/xml');

$URL = 'http://webservicex.net/globalweather.asmx/
   GetWeather?CountryName=United%20States&CityName=';
$city = urlencode($_REQUEST['city']);
$URL .= $city;
$xml = DOMDocument::load($URL);
?>
```

Finally, you configure the saveXML() method to handle the response you receive.

Graphic

You use the following code to configure the method:

echo $xml->saveXML();

Code

```php
<?php
header('Content-Type: text/xml');

$URL = 'http://webservicex.net/globalweather.asmx/
   GetWeather?CountryName=United%20States&CityName=';
$city = urlencode($_REQUEST['city']);
$URL .= $city;
```

129

```
$xml = DOMDocument::load($URL);
echo $xml->saveXML();
?>
```

Having created the proxy and saved it under the name weather_proxy.php, you now want to configure the HTML page and the JavaScript file for your application.

In the HTML page, you add a text box and a button. Next you assign a function, getWeather(), to the onclick event of the button.

Graphic

The code that adds the text box and the button to the page is

Enter a US City: <input type="text" name="city" id="city" />
<input type="button" onclick="getWeather();" value="Lookup Weather" />

Code

```
<html xmlns="http://www.w3.org/1999/xhtml">
  <head>
    <title>Weather for US cities</title>
    <script type="text/javascript" src="weather.js"></script>
  </head>
  <body>
    <form id="weather" name="weather">
    Enter a US City: <input type="text" name="city"
      id="city" />
    <input type="button" onclick="getWeather();"
      value="Lookup Weather" />
    <br /><br />
    </form>
  </body>
</html>
```

You want the getWeather() function to extract and display weather details in a tabular format. So you also add a table element to the HTML page.

Graphic

The code for the table element is

<table id="weatherOutput"></table>

Code

```
<html xmlns="http://www.w3.org/1999/xhtml">
  <head>
    <title>Weather for US cities</title>
    <script type="text/javascript" src="weather.js"></script>
  </head>
```

130

```
<body>
  <form id="weather" name="weather">
  Enter a US City: <input type="text" name="city"
    id="city" />
  <input type="button" onclick="getWeather();"
    value="Lookup Weather" />
  <br /><br />
  <table id="weatherOutput"></table>
  </form>
</body>
</html>
```

You're now configuring the getWeather() function in the JavaScript file. In this function, you first clear the result of the previous query using the abort() method and then you create a query for the proxy file.

Graphic

To accomplish these two tasks, you use the following code:

ajax.abort();
  var url = "weather_proxy.php?city="
  + document.weather.city.value;

Code

```
var ajax = null;
if (window.XMLHttpRequest)
{
  ajax = new XMLHttpRequest();
} else if (window.ActiveXObject)
{
  ajax = new ActiveXObject("Microsoft.XMLHTTP");
}

function getWeather()
{
  ajax.abort();
  var url = "weather_proxy.php?city="
    + document.weather.city.value;
}
```

Next you pass on the query to the open() method.

Graphic

The code to do this is

ajax.open("GET", url, true);

Code

131

```
var ajax = null;
if (window.XMLHttpRequest)
{
  ajax = new XMLHttpRequest();
} else if (window.ActiveXObject)
{
  ajax = new ActiveXObject("Microsoft.XMLHTTP");
}

function getWeather()
{
  ajax.abort();
  var url = "weather_proxy.php?city="
    + document.weather.city.value;
  ajax.open("GET", url, true);
}
```

You then assign the showWeather() function to process the responses sent by the proxy. You also configure the send() method to send the value null since we use the GET command.

Graphic

The code for these two tasks is

ajax.onreadystatechange = showWeather;
  ajax.send(null);

Code

```
var ajax = null;
if (window.XMLHttpRequest)
{
  ajax = new XMLHttpRequest();
} else if (window.ActiveXObject)
{
  ajax = new ActiveXObject("Microsoft.XMLHTTP");
}

function getWeather()
{
  ajax.abort();
  var url = "weather_proxy.php?city="
    + document.weather.city.value;
  ajax.open("GET", url, true);
  ajax.onreadystatechange = showWeather;
  ajax.send(null);
}
```

The file retrieved by the proxy is stored as a read-only object. So you configure the showWeather() function to pass on this object to a variable. You can then extract XML data from the variable.

Graphic

The code to pass on the read-only object to a variable is

var XML = ajax.responseXML;

Code

```
if (window.XMLHttpRequest)
{
  ajax = new XMLHttpRequest();
} else if (window.ActiveXObject)
{
  ajax = new ActiveXObject("Microsoft.XMLHTTP");
}

function getWeather()
{
  ajax.abort();
  var url = "weather_proxy.php?city="
    + document.weather.city.value;
  ajax.open("GET", url, true);
  ajax.onreadystatechange = showWeather;
  ajax.send(null);
}

function showWeather()
{
  if (ajax.readyState == 4)
  {
    var XML = ajax.responseXML;
  }
}
```

You want to store the extracted XML data in a variable named xmlDoc. So you also declare this document variable in the showWeather() function. Additionally, you declare another variable named xmlObject.

Graphic

The code to declare the two variables is

var xmlDoc = null;
var xmlObject = null;

Code

```
  ajax = new XMLHttpRequest();
} else if (window.ActiveXObject)
{
  ajax = new ActiveXObject("Microsoft.XMLHTTP");
}

function getWeather()
```

133

```
  {
    ajax.abort();
    var url = "weather_proxy.php?city="
      + document.weather.city.value;
    ajax.open("GET", url, true);
    ajax.onreadystatechange = showWeather;
    ajax.send(null);
  }

  function showWeather()
  {
    if (ajax.readyState == 4)
    {
      var XML = ajax.responseXML;
      var xmlDoc = null;
      var xmlObject = null;
    }
  }
```

You now want to ensure that the XML data is correctly parsed and doesn't contain whitespace or
<string> tags. Because this depends on the browser being used, you configure parsing for Internet
Explorer and Mozilla-based browsers separately.

Code

```
    ajax.send(null);
  }

  function showWeather()
  {
    if (ajax.readyState == 4)
    {
      var XML = ajax.responseXML;
      var xmlDoc = null;
      var xmlObject = null;

      if (window.ActiveXObject)
      {
                                    .firstChild.nodeValue;
        xmlobject = new ActiveXObject("Microsoft.XMLDOM")
        xmlObject.async="false";
        xmlObject.           (xmlDoc);
      } else
      {
                                    .firstChild.nodeValue;
        var xmlParser = new DOMParser();
        xmlObject= xmlParser.                  (xmlDoc, "text/xml");
      }
    }
  }
```

In Internet Explorer browsers, the XML data is stored in childNodes[1]. *So you add code to extract this data and store it in the* xmlDoc *variable.*

You use the loadXML() *method to store the* xmlDoc *variable in* xmlObject, *an ActiveXObject instance.*

For Mozilla-based browsers, you configure the xmlDoc *variable to store data extracted from* childNodes[0].

You use the parseFromString() *method to remove the* <string> *tags from the XML content extracted from Mozilla-based browsers. This method belongs to the* DOMParser *object, which you've already declared.*

Finally, you configure the showWeather() function to create the required table.

In this table, you want to extract and display the text stored in three tags – Location, Time, and SkyConditions. So you assign this text to three table cells. And to extract the text from the document stored in xmlObject, you specify a function named getWeatherItem().

Graphic

The code for the table is

```
var table = document.getElementById('weatherOutput');
var row = table.insertRow(table.rows.length);

var cell1 = row.insertCell(row.cells.length);
cell1.appendChild(getWeatherItem("Location", xmlObject));

var cell2 = row.insertCell(row.cells.length);
cell2.appendChild(getWeatherItem("Time", xmlObject));

var cell3 = row.insertCell(row.cells.length);
cell3.appendChild(getWeatherItem("SkyConditions", xmlObject));

table.setAttribute("border", "3");
```

Code

```
  xmlDoc = XML.childNodes[1].firstChild.nodeValue;
  xmlobject = new ActiveXObject("Microsoft.XMLDOM")
  xmlObject.async="false";
  xmlObject.loadXML(xmlDoc);
} else
{
  xmlDoc = XML.childNodes[0].firstChild.nodeValue;
  var xmlParser = new DOMParser();
  xmlObject= xmlParser.parseFromString(xmlDoc, "text/xml");
}
var table = document.getElementById('weatherOutput');
var row = table.insertRow(table.rows.length);
```

```
        var cell1 = row.insertCell(row.cells.length);
        cell1.appendChild(getWeatherItem("Location", xmlObject));

        var cell2 = row.insertCell(row.cells.length);
        cell2.appendChild(getWeatherItem("Time", xmlObject));

        var cell3 = row.insertCell(row.cells.length);
        cell3.appendChild(getWeatherItem("SkyConditions", xmlObject));

        table.setAttribute("border", "3");
    }
}
```

To complete the JavaScript coding, you configure the getWeatherItem() function.

Code

```
    cell1.appendChild(getWeatherItem("Location", xmlObject));

    var cell2 = row.insertCell(row.cells.length);
    cell2.appendChild(getWeatherItem("Time", xmlObject));

    var cell3 = row.insertCell(row.cells.length);
    cell3.appendChild(getWeatherItem("SkyConditions", xmlObject));

    table.setAttribute("border", "3");
    }
}

function getWeatherItem(name, xmlObject)
{
            = xmlObject.getElementsByTagName(name);
    var textNode = null;

    if (window.ActiveXObject)
    {
      textNode = document.                  (tags[0].firstChild.text);
    } else
    {
      textNode = document.                  (tags[0].firstChild.textContent);
    }
                    ;

}
```

You want this function to first search for a tag specified by the showWeather() *function. In* xmlObject, *this tag is identified by its* name *element. So you configure the* getElementsByTagName() *method to extract the* name *element and store it in the* tags *variable.*

Using the createTextNode() *method, you create a new node based on the text extracted from the* tags *variable. You configure this method to work with both Internet Explorer and Mozilla-based browsers.*

You return the textNode *variable, which stores the extracted text, to the* showWeather() *function.*

Question

To consume a web service in your Ajax application, you've created an ASP.NET–based proxy. You're now configuring a function, getAlerts(), in the JavaScript file for the application. You want this function to send user input to the proxy and receive an XML document in response.

Identify the other tasks this function should perform.

Code

```
var ajax = null;
if (window.XMLHttpRequest)
{
  ajax = new XMLHttpRequest();
} else if (window.ActiveXObject)
{
  ajax = new ActiveXObject("Microsoft.XMLHTTP");
}

function getAlerts()
{
  var url = "weather_proxy.php?city=" +
    document.alerts.city.value;
  ajax.onreadystatechange = showAlerts;
}
```

Options:

1. Clear the results of any previous query
2. Pass on the query to the open() method
3. Create an instance of the XmlDocument object
4. Use the InnerXml property to handle the response

Answer

Option 1: This option is correct. The function should be able to clear the results generated by previous queries. To ensure this, you add the abort() *method to the function.*

Option 2: This option is correct. The function should pass on the query to the open() *method. This method, in turn, passes on the query to the proxy.*

Option 3: This option is incorrect. The XmlDocument *object should be part of the ASP.NET proxy. This object enables the proxy to extract XML data from the web service.*

Option 4: This option is incorrect. The proxy uses the InnerXml *property to store the data it retrieves from the web service. You don't need to add this property to the JavaScript function.*

1. Clear the results of any previous query
2. Pass on the query to the open() method

3. Using a tag to consume a web service

When calling a web service, if you want to completely avoid creating any server-side code, you can use a <script> tag hack.

With this technique, you can call a web service using the <script> tag's src attribute. You configure this attribute in the JavaScript code for your application.

You don't need to configure the XMLHttpRequest object when using the <script> tag hack. This makes the technique very simple to use.

The only constraint to this technique is that your web service should send its response in the JavaScript Object Notation, commonly known as JSON, format. You can't extract XML data with this technique.

Suppose you want to integrate the Yahoo! Image Search Web Service with an Ajax web page. This web service sends data in JSON format. So you decide to use the <script> tag hack to consume the service.

However, before you configure the <script> tag hack in the JavaScript file, you want to create a user interface for the web service. So you add a text box and a button to the Ajax page. Additionally, you associate a function named script_hack() with the onclick event of the button.

Graphic

The code for the text box and the button is

Enter a search term: <input type="text" name="query" id="query" />
<input type="button" onclick="script_hack();" value="Find Images" />

Code

```
<html xmlns="http://www.w3.org/1999/xhtml">
 <head>
  <title>Yahoo Image Search</title>
  <script type="text/javascript" src="search.js"></script>
 </head>
 <body>
  <form id="search" name="search">
  Enter a search term: <input type="text" name="query"
   id="query" />
  <input type="button" onclick="script_hack();"
   value="Find Images" />
  <br /><br />
  <table id="output"></table>
  </form>
 </body>
</html>
```

You're now configuring the script_hack() function in the JavaScript file. You start by assigning the image-retrieval query to a variable named url. This query contains the user-specified search criteria.

Graphic

To assign the query, you use the following code:

url = "http://search.yahooapis.com/ImageSearchService/
V1/imageSearch?appid=YahooDemo&query="
+document.search.query.value;

Code

```
function parseOutput(JSON)
{
  alert(JSON.ResultSet.totalResultsAvailable+"
  results were found for your search");
}

function script_hack()
{
  url = "http://search.yahooapis.com/ImageSearchService/
    V1/imageSearch?appid=YahooDemo&
    query="+document.search.query.value;
}
```

To ensure that the query returns only JSON data, you then set the output attribute.

Graphic

The code to do this is

output=json

Code

```
function parseOutput(JSON)
{
  alert(JSON.ResultSet.totalResultsAvailable+"
  results were found for your search");
}

function script_hack()
{
  url = "http://search.yahooapis.com/ImageSearchService/
    V1/imageSearch?appid=YahooDemo&output=json&
    query="+document.search.query.value;
}
```

And to ensure that the secondary function, parseOutput(), is called after the query returns a response, you set the callback attribute. The parseOutput() function alerts users about the total number of search results retrieved by script_hack().

Graphic

The code for this is

callback=parseOutput

Code

```
function parseOutput(JSON)
{
  alert(JSON.ResultSet.totalResultsAvailable+"
  results were found for your search");
}

function script_hack()
{
  url = "http://search.yahooapis.com/ImageSearchService/
    V1/imageSearch?appid=YahooDemo&output=json&
    callback=parseOutput&
    query="+document.search.query.value;
}
```

You next add the <script> tag hack.

Code

```
function parseOutput(JSON)
{
  alert(JSON.ResultSet.totalResultsAvailable+"
  results were found for your search");
}

function script_hack()
{
  url = "http://search.yahooapis.com/ImageSearchService/
    V1/imageSearch?appid=YahooDemo&output=json&
    callback=parseOutput&
    query="+document.search.query.value;
  var head = document.                              .item(0);
  var script = document.              ("script");
  script.              ("type", "text/javascript");
  script.              ("src", url);
  head.              (script);
}
```

You use the getElementsByTagName() *method to extract the* head *element from the web page. This helps you to access the* script *tag in the web page.*

Using the createElement() *method, you create a JavaScript version of the* script *tag. You save this version as a variable named* script.

With the setAttribute() *method, you set the* type *and* src *attributes for the* script *variable. The first action ensures that the* script *variable can recognize JavaScript code. The second assigns the image-retrieval query to the* src *attribute.*

Using the appendChild() *method, you add the* script *variable to the* head *element. This ensures that the web page can use the* src *attribute of the* script *variable to call the web service.*

Although useful, the application proxy and <script> tag hacks each have their drawbacks. Whereas the first requires server-side code, the second allows you to retrieve only JSON data. Also, you need to write complex JavaScript code if you want your Ajax applications to work correctly in all types of browsers. To overcome these drawbacks, several new solutions have been proposed.

These solutions include

creating a new header

According to researcher Chris Holland, Ajax developers can create a new type of header to consume web services. This header is named Allow Foreign Hands. When used in conjunction with an object named ContextAgnosticXMLHttpRequest, this header allows access to web services across multiple domains.

using Flash, and

Flash can access web services across multiple domains using a file named crossdomain.xml. This file contains a list of approved domains. Researchers propose to use Flash to call web services hosted on these domains from Ajax applications. To do this, they've created an object named FlashXMLHttpRequest.

creating a new browser service

JSONRequest is a new browser service that can allow applications to directly access JSON format data. With this service, you won't have to convert JSON data to XML first.

Question

You want to integrate a web service with your Ajax application. This web service returns data in JSON format.

Which steps should you take when configuring the JavaScript code for the application?

Code

```
<html xmlns="http://www.w3.org/1999/xhtml">
  <head>
    <title>Hotel Search</title>
```

```
      <script type="text/javascript" src="search.js"></script>
      </head>
      <body>
       <form id="search" name="search">
       Enter a search term: <input type="text" name="query"
        id="query" />
       <input type="button" onclick="function();"
        value="Find Hotels" />
       <br /><br />
       <table id="output"></table>
       </form>
       </body>
      </html>
```

Options:

1. Assign each user request to the src attribute
2. Create a node to store data sent by the web service
3. Extract the head element from the web page
4. Append the head element to the response you receive

Answer

Option 1: This option is correct. If a web service returns JSON data, you can send queries to the service by using the <script> tag's src attribute.

Option 2: This option is incorrect. The web service sends data in JSON format. You don't need to create a node to store this data.

Option 3: This option is correct. To access the script tag from the JavaScript code, you first need to extract the head element to the code.

Option 4: This option is incorrect. You append the head element to the JavaScript version of the script tag. This enables you to use the tag's src attribute to send queries.

Correct answer(s):

1. Assign each user request to the src attribute
3. Extract the head element from the web page

Summary

If you want to quickly add complex features to your Ajax applications, you should consider using web services. A web service is a functional add-on that contains all the code required to perform specific tasks. You only need to call the web service from your application to use its features. Many web services are freely available on the Internet.

To call or consume a web service, you can use various techniques. For example, if the service is located in the same domain as your application, you can use the XMLHttpRequest object to consume it. Otherwise, you can use workarounds such as using application proxies and configuring the <script> tags.

Ajax APIs and Mashups

Learning Objectives

After completing this topic, you should be able to

- *create an application to use an API*
- *create a mashup*

1. Adding an API to an Ajax application

Just as you can consume web services in your Ajax applications, you can also add APIs to them. An API allows you to integrate sections of another web site, such as Google Maps, into your applications. These integrated sections are fully functional. Each API uses methods and queries to retrieve information from its parent web site and display the information via the integrated sections.

Many web portals, including Twitter and Facebook, offer free APIs. You can use these APIs to add the features and functions of the web portals to your Ajax application.

The following are some commonly used APIs:

- Google AJAX APIs
  The URL is

  http://code.google.com/apis/ajax

- Twitter APIs
  The URL is

  http://apiwiki.twitter.com/

- eBay APIs, and
  The URL is

  http://developer.ebay.com/

- Facebook APIs
  The URL is

  http://developers.facebook.com/

Note

You can access http://www.programmableweb.com/apis to find a repository of APIs. This web page offers links to APIs created by a wide variety of web portals.

APIs present content in a manner similar to web services. However, APIs have a few inherent differences:

flexibility regarding data exchange techniques and

Unlike web services, APIs are flexible regarding data exchange techniques. For example, a web service accepts queries in the form of HTTP GET or POST statements or SOAP documents. And it sends back XML or SOAP documents in response. By contrast, an API uses a collection of methods to exchange information with its parent web site. These methods can be in a variety of languages, such as C# or JavaScript.

An API can also use web services or TCP/IP commands to exchange information. Each company or web portal that offers an API can implement its own rule for data exchange. So you may have to learn new techniques when using a new API.

the need for registration

Before you can use an API in your Ajax application, you need to register at the parent web site. To register, you normally have to create an account at the web site and obtain an access key. You can access the API from your application only after you add the access key to its HTML page.

Suppose you're creating a web site for NorthGlenn Fitness, a chain of fitness clubs. You want to enable users to quickly locate a branch of NorthGlenn Fitness. To do so, you want to add Google Maps to the home page, using the Google Maps API.

To successfully use the Google Maps API, you need four main components:

- an API key

- a map object

- a Google-provided latitude-longitude converter, and

- an XMLHttpRequest factory method

The API key enables your page to access the web server that hosts the Google Maps API. To receive this key, you only need to sign up for the API. So you browse to this sign-up page.

Graphic

The Sign Up for the Google Maps API page is open. The URL of the page is

http://code.google.com/apis/maps/signup.html

Note

You must have a Google account to sign up.

Next, on the sign-up page, you review and accept the terms and conditions and specify the domain name for the NorthGlenn Fitness web site. The key will be valid for this domain name and its constituent subdomains and folders.

Graphic

The Sign Up for the Google Maps API page displays the I have read and agree with the terms and conditions checkbox, the My web site URL text box, and the Generate API Key button. The checkbox is selected, and the text box displays the URL http://www.northglenn.org.

You can also generate a key for an application that you host on your local computer. For this, you need to specify the localhost address in the My web site URL box.

To generate the key, you now click the **Generate API Key** button.

If you aren't already signed into your Google account, you are taken to the sign in page when you click the **Generate API Key** *button.*

The Sign Up for the Google Maps API page specifies your access key and explains how you should use the key. For example, when using the JavaScript version of the API, you should add the access key to the HTML file for your web page.

Graphic

The Sign Up for the Google Maps API page contains a section named Thank You for Signing Up for a Google Maps API Key and a subsection named JavaScript Maps API Example.

You want to use JavaScript code to exchange requests and responses with the API. So you decide to use the JavaScript version of the API.

You're now configuring the HTML file for the home page.

This involves the following initial steps:

Code

```
<html xmlns="http://www.w3.org/1999/xhtml">
  <head>
    <title>NorthGlenn Fitness Clubs</title>
  </head>
  <body>
  </body>
</html>
```

1. specifying the URL of the JavaScript file that contains details about the Google Maps API
    The code to do this is
    src="http://maps.google.com/maps?file=api&v=2

Code
```
<html xmlns="http://www.w3.org/1999/xhtml">
  <head>
    <title>NorthGlenn Fitness Clubs</title>
    <script src="http://maps.google.com/maps?file=api&v=2
    type="text/javascript"></script>
  </head>
  <body>
```

```
    </body>
</html>
```

- adding the access key via the key attribute
  The code is

  *&key=ABQIAAAACdOwtcjE0jj84z2XJkA13RQip0Pesw10x1Dhb_g8PH38rls6GhTvdTi1zvznlqW9tF7Hxk
  96f54WcA"*

  Code
  ```
  <html xmlns="http://www.w3.org/1999/xhtml">
    <head>
      <title>NorthGlenn Fitness Clubs</title>
      <script src="http://maps.google.com/maps?file=api&v=2
      &key=ABQIAAAACdOwtcjE0jj84z2XJkA13RQip0Pesw1
      Ox1Dhb_g8PH38rls6GhTvdTi1zvznlqW9tF7Hxk96f54WcA"
      type="text/javascript"></script>
    </head>
    <body>
    </body>
  </html>
  ```

- adding a reference to the external JavaScript file, which you plan to use to exchange data with the API, and
  The code to do this is

  <script type="text/javascript" src="map.js"></script>

  Code
  ```
  <html xmlns="http://www.w3.org/1999/xhtml">
    <head>
      <title>NorthGlenn Fitness Clubs</title>
      <script src="http://maps.google.com/maps?file=api&v=2
      &key=ABQIAAAACdOwtcjE0jj84z2XJkA13RQip0Pesw1
      Ox1Dhb_g8PH38rls6GhTvdTi1zvznlqW9tF7Hxk96f54WcA"
      type="text/javascript"></script>
      <script type="text/javascript" src="map.js"></script>
    </head>
    <body>
    </body>
  </html>
  ```

- adding a text box that allows users to specify the name of the city and state where they want to locate a fitness club
  The code for this is

  <input id="address" name="address" type="text" size="50" />

  Code
  ```
  <html xmlns="http://www.w3.org/1999/xhtml">
    <head>
      <title>NorthGlenn Fitness Clubs</title>
  ```

```
          <script src="http://maps.google.com/maps?file=api&v=2
          &key=ABQIAAAACdOwtcjE0jj84z2XJkA13RQip0Pesw1
          Ox1Dhb_g8PH38rls6GhTvdTi1zvznlqW9tF7Hxk96f54WcA"
          type="text/javascript"></script>
          <script type="text/javascript" src="map.js"></script>
      </head>
      <body>
      <input id="address" name="address" type="text" size="50" />
      </body>
  </html>
```

Having added the access key, you now need to create a map object in the map.js file. This object allows you to embed a portion of Google Maps on the home page. You can then configure markers to identify the user-specified addresses on the map.

But before you configure the map object, you allocate space for it on the home page using the div element.

Graphic

The code to create the map object is

<div id="map" style="width: 500px; height: 300px;"></div>

Code

```
<html xmlns="http://www.w3.org/1999/xhtml">
  <head>
    <title>NorthGlenn Fitness Clubs</title>
    <script src="http://maps.google.com/maps?file=api&v=2
    &key=ABQIAAAACdOwtcjE0jj84z2XJkA13RQip0Pesw1
    Ox1Dhb_g8PH38rls6GhTvdTi1zvznlqW9tF7Hxk96f54WcA"
    type="text/javascript"></script>
    <script type="text/javascript" src="map.js"></script>
  </head>
  <body>
  <input id="address" name="address" type="text" size="50" />
  <div id="map" style="width: 500px; height: 300px;"></div>
  </body>
</html>
```

You also add two Google-provided JavaScript functions – load() and GUnload().

You can use the load() function to create the desired map object. You need to manually specify this function in the map.js file. To ensure that your home page can launch this function, you add this function to the onclick event of a button.

After a user stops using a map object, you can use the preconfigured GUnload() function to delete the object. This helps prevent memory leaks. You can't further customize the code for the GUnload() function.

Graphic

The code add the two functions is

<body onload="load()" onunload="GUnload()">

And the code for the button that launches the load() function is

<input type="button" onclick="load('true');" value="Go!" />

Code

```
<html xmlns="http://www.w3.org/1999/xhtml">
  <head>
    <title>NorthGlenn Fitness Clubs</title>
    <script src="http://maps.google.com/maps?file=api&v=2
    &key=ABQIAAAACdOwtcjE0jj84z2XJkA13RQip0Pesw1
    Ox1Dhb_g8PH38rls6GhTvdTi1zvznIqW9tF7Hxk96f54WcA"
    type="text/javascript"></script>
    <script type="text/javascript" src="map.js"></script>
  </head>
  <body onload="load()" onunload="GUnload()">
  <input id="address" name="address" type="text" size="50" />
  <input type="button" onclick="load('true');" value="Go!" />
  <div id="map" style="width: 500px; height: 300px;"></div>
  </body>
</html>
```

You're now configuring the load() function. In this function, you first check whether the host browser is compatible with Google Maps. You use the GBrowserIsCompatible() function for this.

Graphic

The code to use the GBrowserIsCompatible() function is

if (GBrowserIsCompatible())

Code

```
var map = null;
var ajax = null;

function load()
{
  if (GBrowserIsCompatible())
  {

  }
}
```

You then use the GMap2 constructor to declare an instance of the Google Maps. To this instance, you pass on the id value of the div element. This ensures that the resultant map stays within the div element.

Graphic

The code the creates the map instance is

map = new GMap2(document.getElementById("map"));

Code

```
var map = null;
var ajax = null;

function load()
{
  if (GBrowserIsCompatible())
  {
    map = new GMap2(document.getElementById("map"));
  }
}
```

Finally, you use the setCenter() method to set the initial state of the map. This ensures that when a user first accesses the map, it is centered on a default location. You specify the latitude and longitude of this location by using the GLatLng() method.

Graphic

The code to set the initial state of the map is

map.setCenter(new GLatLng(39.885541, -104.9872026), 13);

Code

```
var map = null;
var ajax = null;

function load()
{
  if (GBrowserIsCompatible())
  {
    map = new GMap2(document.getElementById("map"));
    map.setCenter(new GLatLng(39.885541, -104.9872026), 13);
  }
}
```

Having set the default location, you now want to ensure that the map can pan to and display markers at the addresses specified by the users. To do this, you need to convert the addresses into latitudes and longitudes. This process is known as *geocoding*. To automate the process, Google provides a converter object named Geocode.

You add code that implements the Geocode converter.

Code

```
function shiftMarker(address)
{
    geocoder = new GClientGeocoder();
    geocoder.getLatLng(address, function(point) {
        if (!point)
        {
            alert(address + "not found");
        } else
        {
            map.setCenter(point, 13);
            var marker = new GMarker(point);
            map.addOverlay(marker);
            marker.openInfoWindowHtml(address);
        }
    });
}
```

GClientGeocoder()

To use the Geocode converter, you first create an instance of the GClientGeocoder object. In the example, this instance is named geocoder. This instance accesses geographical coordinates – latitude and longitude values – from Google servers.

getLatLng

You use the getLatLng() method to convert the addresses into their equivalent geographical coordinates.

function(point)

The function(point) declaration signifies the anonymous function that you need to pass on to the getLatLang() method. You use the point parameter in this function to check whether the user-specified address is valid. If it is, the point parameter contains a latitude-longitude pair. Otherwise, it contains a null value.

setCenter

If the point parameter contains a latitude-longitude pair, you pass on this pair to the setCenter() method. This method ensures that the map is now centered on the new location.

GMarker

To create a marker at the new location, you first declare an instance of the GMarker() object. This instance is named marker. To this instance, you pass on the values stored in the point parameter.

Additionally, you use the addOverlay() method to add the marker instance to the map. And you use the openInfoWindowHtml() method to ensure that details about the selected address appear over the icon of the marker.

Finally, you need to configure the home page to handle Ajax requests and responses. Google provides an XMLHttpRequest factory method, the GXmlHttp namespace, for this. The GXmlHttp namespace creates an XMLHttpRequest instance that is compatible with all types of browsers.

You use a method named create to create a GXmlHttp object. You can then use this object just as you would an XMLHttpRequest instance. The GXmlHttp object recognizes all XMLHttpRequest methods and properties.

Graphic

The code to create a GXmlHttp object is

ajax = GXmlHttp.create();

Code

```
ajax = GXmlHttp.create();
ajax.open("GET", "myfile.xml", true);
ajax.onreadystatechange = function()
{
  if (ajax.readyState == 4)
  {
    alert(ajax.responseXML);
  }
}
ajax.send(null);
```

Alternatively, if you want even more compact code, you can use the GDownloadUrl function instead of the GXmlHttp namespace. The GDownloadUrl function automatically detects whether the required content has been downloaded. You don't need to verify the value of the readyState property in this case.

Code

```
GDownloadUrl("myfile.xml", function(data, responseCode) {
alert(data);
});
```

Case Study: Question 1 of 3

Scenario

For your convenience, the case study is repeated with each question.

Mike is developing an Ajax web page for a travel agency. To enable visitors to search for major tourist attractions, Mike needs to display a portion of Google Maps on the page. So Mike is configuring the HTML and JavaScript files for the web page to use the Google Maps API.

Help Mike correctly configure the two files by answering the questions in order.

Question

Mike has signed up for the Google Maps API and now wants to ensure that the web page can load the API.

What steps should he take?

Code
```
<html xmlns="http://www.w3.org/1999/xhtml">
  <head>
    <title>Easy Nomad Travel</title>

  </head>
```

```
      <body onload="load()" onunload="GUnload()">
      <input id="address" name="address" type="text" size="50" />
      <input type="button" value="Locate Address" />
      <div id="map" style="width: 500px; height: 300px;"></div>
      </body>
</html>
```

Options:

1. Add the API code to the div element in the <body> tag
2. Add the API key to the key attribute of a <script> tag
3. Configure the GUnload() function to load the API and display a map instance
4. Specify the URL of the JavaScript file that contains details about the API

Answer

Option 1: This option is incorrect. The details about the API are stored in a JavaScript file. Mike only needs to specify the URL and the access key for this file. He doesn't need to create code for the API all over again.

Option 2: This option is correct. The API key enables your web page to access details about the API. So Mike should add this key to the HTML file.

Option 3: This option is incorrect. The GUnload() function is preconfigured. Mike doesn't have to manually configure it. He has to configure only the load() function.

Option 4: This option is correct. The details about the Google Maps API are stored in a JavaScript file. To enable his application to use this file, Mike should specify the URL of the file via the <script> tag.

Correct answer(s):

2. Add the API key to the key attribute of a <script> tag
4. Specify the URL of the JavaScript file that contains details about the API

Case Study: Question 2 of 3

Scenario

For your convenience, the case study is repeated with each question.

Mike is developing an Ajax web page for a travel agency. To enable visitors to search for major tourist attractions, Mike needs to display a portion of Google Maps on the page. So Mike is configuring the HTML and JavaScript files for the web page to use the Google Maps API.

Help Mike correctly configure the two files by answering the questions in order.

Question

Mike has added a Google Map instance to the web page. He now wants to add a marker that points out a user-specified address on the map.

To ensure that the address is converted into its equivalent geographical coordinates, he is configuring a function named displayMarker. He has already supplied the user-specified address variable to this function.

What code should he now add to the function?

Code

```
var map = new GMap2(document.getElementById("map"));
// additional code

function displayMarker(address)
{
    var converter = INSERT THE MISSING CODE
    converter.getLatLng(address, function(point) {
        if (!point)
        {
            alert(address + "not found");
        } else
        {
            map.setCenter(point, 13);
            // additional code
            map.addOverlay(marker);
            marker.openInfoWindowHtml(address);
        }
    });
}
```

Options:

1. new GClientGeocoder();
2. new GMarker();
3. new GLatLng(point);

Answer

Option 1: This option is correct. Mike should declare an instance of the GClientGeocoder() object. This instance can retrieve geographical coordinates from Google servers.

Option 2: This option is incorrect. The GMarker() object only adds a marker at the user-specified address on the map. It doesn't convert the address into its equivalent geographical coordinates.

Option 3: This option is incorrect. Using the GLatLng() method, Mike can only set the latitude and longitude for a specific address. He can't use this method to convert random addresses.

Correct answer(s):

1. new GClientGeocoder();

Case Study: Question 3 of 3

Scenario

For your convenience, the case study is repeated with each question.

Mike is developing an Ajax web page for a travel agency. To enable visitors to search for major tourist attractions, Mike needs to display a portion of Google Maps on the page. So Mike is configuring the HTML and JavaScript files for the web page to use the Google Maps API.

Help Mike correctly configure the two files by answering the questions in order.

Question

Mike is now configuring the web page to retrieve XML files from the server. When doing so, he wants to use a single object to handle requests and responses for any type of browser.

What actions should he perform?

Options:

1. Create an instance of the XMLHttpRequest object
2. Configure an instance of the GXmlHttp namespace
3. Call the methods and properties of the XMLHttpRequest object
4. Create new functions that allow cross-browser compatibility

Answer

Option 1: This option is incorrect. The XMLHttpRequest *object cannot exchange information with browsers based on Internet Explorer 6 or its earlier versions.*

Option 2: This option is correct. An GXmlHttp *object offers cross-browser compatibility.*

Option 3: This option is correct. When using a GXmlHttp *object, Mike can use all the methods and properties of* XMLHttpRequest.

Option 4: This option is incorrect. Mike doesn't need to create new functions when using the GXmlHttp *object. He can reuse the* XMLHttpRequest *methods and properties.*

Correct answer(s):

2. Configure an instance of the GXmlHttp namespace
3. Call the methods and properties of the XMLHttpRequest object

2. Creating a mashup

In an Ajax application, you can use multiple APIs and web services to create an entirely new service. For example, you can combine the Google Maps API with a traffic-update widget to create a new service that provides information on the number of users accessing your web page from different locations. This type of service is called a *mashup*.

When creating a mashup, you transfer content from one or more APIs or web services to an XML document. You then retrieve and display relevant content from this document via another API or web service. You use the XMLHttpRequest object to facilitate the transfer and retrieval of the content.

Graphic

154

Suppose you want to add a mashup to a web application you're creating for a travel agency. You want this mashup to display photos against specific locations on an embedded Google Maps instance. To download the photos, you want to use an API offered by Flickr, a photo-sharing web site.

Before you can use the Flickr API in your application, you need to register for the API using this page.

Graphic

The URL of the page is

http://www.flickr.com/services/api/keys/apply/

During the registration process, you first need to log on to Flickr using your Yahoo! account. Then, you need to apply for an API key. This key allows potential users of your application to directly use the services of the API.

If you want users to have to log on to Flickr before they can use the API services, you need to follow another process:

1. apply for the API key

2. create a link, using the API key, that accepts logon credentials

3. create a handler that validates the credentials

4. use the handler to call the getToken() method and create a token

5. use the token to generate an API call that requires authentication, and

6. add the API call to your application

Having obtained an API key from the Flickr web site, you now want to download photos. To do this, you can use the source URL of each photo.

A source URL is dynamic and can have this format.

Syntax

http://static.flickr.com/{server-id}/{id}_{secret}_[mstb].jpg

The {server-id} attribute specifies the ID of the server on which the photo is stored.

The ID of the photo you want to retrieve replaces the {id} attribute.

The {secret} attribute refers to the Flickr-assigned secret key associated with the photo.

You can use one of four letters – m, s, t, or b – to specify the dimensions of the photo. For example, if you want to display a small, 75x75 pixels, photo, you can replace [mstb] in the URL with the letter s.

Similarly, the letter m signifies a photo that measures 240 pixels on the longest side, while the letter t signifies a thumbnail that measures 100 pixels on the longest side. And the letter b signifies a large photo, which is 1024 pixels on the longest side.

To download a photo to your application, you need to pass on the source URL of the photo to the application's JavaScript file. However, before you configure the JavaScript file, you want to set up the HTML file for the application.

In the HTML file, you add an access key for the Google Maps API. You also allocate space for a Google Maps instance. But you don't add any text boxes or buttons to the file. This is to ensure that Flickr photos are displayed only for the locations you specify.

Code

```html
<html xmlns="http://www.w3.org/1999/xhtml">
 <head>
  <meta http-equiv="content-type" content="text/html";
   charset=utf-8" />
  <title>Easy Nomad Location</title>
  <script src="http://maps.google.com/maps?file=api&v=2
   &key=ABQIAAAAZUgQcERqJbKFRuoDh0HM7RT1gBj71UlO4u1
   BPAtlju0eWgO2gBS2OLMRSnXcXKNJ_WLBJNvqZBVlhQ"
   type="text/javascript"></script>
  <script type="text/javascript" src="map.js"></script>
 </head>
 <body onload="load();">
  <div id="map" style="width: 500px; height: 300px;"></div>
 </body>
</html>
```

You next create two other files:

Code

```xml
<?xml version="1.0"?>
<locations>
 <location lat="48.85359" lng="2.292366" address="c" />
 <location lat="48.880634" lng="2.282752" address="h" />
</locations>
```

- locations.xml, which specifies the locations for which you want to display photos and

  Code
  ```xml
  <?xml version="1.0"?>
  <locations>
   <location lat="48.85359" lng="2.292366" address="c" />
   <location lat="48.880634" lng="2.282752" address="h" />
  </locations>
  ```

- updateXml.php, a proxy that you'll use to download content from Flickr

  Code
  ```php
  <?php

  header("Content-Type: text/xml");
  ```

156

```php
$url = "http://api.flickr.com/services/rest/?method=";
$method = $_REQUEST['api'];
$api_key = $_REQUEST['key'];
$param_key = $_REQUEST['param_key'];
$param_value = $_REQUEST['param_value'];
$url .= $method.'&api_key='.$api_key.'&'.$param_key.
   '='.$param_value.'&per_page=1&page=1';
$url = DOMDocument::load($url);
$XML = $url->saveXML();
echo $XML;
?>
```

You now move on to configuring the JavaScript file.

To begin with, you declare the load() function in the file. In this function, you use the getLatLng() method to set a city name as the default location on the embedded map.

Graphic

The code to set the default location to Washington is

geocoder.getLatLng("Washington", function(point)
{map.setCenter(point, 13)});

Code

```javascript
var map = null;
var geocoder = null;

function load(e)
{
 if (GBrowserIsCompatible())
 {
  map = new GMap2(document.getElementById("map"));
  geocoder = new GClientGeocoder();
  geocoder.getLatLng("Washington", function(point)
   {map.setCenter(point, 13)});
  placeMarkers();
 }
}
```

You also call another function, placeMarkers(). If a user clicks any of the locations specified in locations.xml on the map, this function will place a marker on the location. The function will also download a photo related to the location from Flickr and display the photo next to the marker.

Graphic

The code to call the function is

placeMarkers();

Code

```
var map = null;
var geocoder = null;

function load(e)
{
  if (GBrowserIsCompatible())
  {
    map = new GMap2(document.getElementById("map"));
    geocoder = new GClientGeocoder();
    geocoder.getLatLng("Washington", function(point)
      {map.setCenter(point, 13)});
    placeMarkers();
  }
}
```

Before you begin configuring the placeMarkers() function, you declare another function named getImageURL(). You want to use this function to download photos from Flickr.

To ensure that the photos are related to the addresses specified in locations.xml, you pass on the address variable to the function. You then configure the function to pass on the source URLs of the photos to Flickr.

Code

```
  if (GBrowserIsCompatible())
  {
    map = new GMap2(document.getElementById("map"));
    geocoder = new GClientGeocoder();
    geocoder.getLatLng("Washington", function(point)
      {map.setCenter(point, 13)});
    placeMarkers();
  }
}

function getImageURL(address)
{
  GDownloadUrl("updateXml.php?api=flickr.photos.search
    &key=5794g9te45lll2766n554vx0a941f5d6&param_key=text
    &param_value="+address, function(data, responseCode) {
  var xml = GXml.parse(data);
  var photos = xml.documentElement.getElementsByTagName("photo");
  var server = photos[0].getAttribute("server");
  var id = photos[0].getAttribute("id");
  var secret = photos[0].getAttribute("secret");
  var imageUrl = "http://static.flickr.com/"+server+"/"
    +id+"_"+secret+"_s.jpg";
  alert (imageUrl);
  })
}
```

```
GDownloadUrl
```

158

The GDownloadUrl() *function enables you to asynchronously retrieve the photos from Flickr. You first pass in a* *query for the flickr.php file to this function. You attach the Flickr access key to the query by using the* key *attribute. You also attach the* address *variable and an anonymous function to the query.*

GXml.parse

To ensure that the anonymous function can parse the XML data returned by Flickr, you use the parse() *method* *of the GXml namespace.*

var server = photos[0].getAttribute("server");
var id = photos[0].getAttribute("id");
var secret = photos[0].getAttribute("secret");

In the anonymous function, you also declare three variables – server, id, and secret. *You configure these* *variables to extract the values stored in the* server, id, *and* secret *attributes for the photos. These attributes are* *part of the parsed XML DOM.*

var imageUrl

The imageUrl *variable in the anonymous function contains the source URL of the photo to be downloaded. This* *URL extracts values from the* server, id, *and* secret *variables. It also uses the* s *attribute to ensure that the* *downloaded photo is sized to 75x75 pixels.*

You're now configuring the placeMarkers() function. You first declare the GDownloadUrl function to asynchronously retrieve content from the locations.xml file. You also create a for loop that generates markers on the embedded map based on the lat and lng values specified in locations.xml.

Graphic

The code configured in the placeMarkers() function is

```
GDownloadUrl("locations.xml", function(data, responseCode) {
var xml = GXml.parse(data);
var markers = xml.documentElement.getElementsByTagName("location");
for (var i=0; i<markers.length; i++)
 {
   point2 = new GLatLng(parseFloat(markers[i].getAttribute("lat")),
    parseFloat(markers[i].getAttribute("lng")));
```

Code

```
function getImageURL(address)
{
  GDownloadUrl("updateXml.php?api=flickr.photos.search
   &key=5794g9te45lll2766n554vx0a941f5d6&param_key=text
   &param_value="+address, function(data, responseCode) {
  var xml = GXml.parse(data);
  var photos = xml.documentElement.getElementsByTagName("photo");
  var server = photos[0].getAttribute("server");
  var id = photos[0].getAttribute("id");
  var secret = photos[0].getAttribute("secret");
  var imageUrl = "http://static.flickr.com/"+server+"/"
   +id+"_"+secret+"_s.jpg";
  alert (imageUrl);
```

```
  })
}
```

```
function placeMarkers(address, e)
{
  GDownloadUrl("locations.xml", function(data, responseCode) {
  var xml = GXml.parse(data);
  var markers = xml.documentElement.getElementsByTagName("location");
  for (var i=0; i<markers.length; i++)
  {
    point2 = new GLatLng(parseFloat(markers[i].getAttribute("lat")),
      parseFloat(markers[i].getAttribute("lng")));
```

To complete the JavaScript coding, you add a few more elements to the placeMarkers() function.

Code

```
}

function placeMarkers(address, e)
{
  GDownloadUrl("locations.xml", function(data, responseCode) {
  var xml = GXml.parse(data);
  var markers = xml.documentElement.getElementsByTagName("location");
  for (var i=0; i<markers.length; i++)
  {
    point2 = new GLatLng(parseFloat(markers[i].getAttribute("lat")),
      parseFloat(markers[i].getAttribute("lng")));
    map.setCenter(point2, 13);
    map.setZoom(3);
    marker2 = new GMarker(point2);
    map.addOverlay(marker2);
    var imageUrl = getImageURL(markers[i].getAttribute("address"));
    alert(imageUrl);
    GEvent.addListener(marker2,"click",
      (function (marker, pImageurl) {
       return function() { marker.openInfoWindowHtml
       ("<img src='"+pImageurl+"' />", new GSize(200,200)); }
      })(marker2, imageUrl));
  }
})
}
```

> map.setCenter(point2, 13);
> map.setZoom(3);
> marker2 = new GMarker(point2);

You use the setCenter() *method to center the map on the location specified by the* point2 *variable, the* setZoom() *method to zoom in on the location, and the* GMarker() *object to create a marker.*

> var imageUrl

Using the imageUrl *variable, you extract the photo returned by the* getImageURL() *function.*

> GEvent.addListener

If a user clicks a marker, you assign the addListener() *method of the* GEvent *namespace to handle the event. Using this method, you also call the* openInfoWindowHtml() *method.*

`openInfoWindowHtml`

With the openInfoWindowHtml() *method, you ensure that the correct photo appears over a marker. To specify the photo, you pass on the* img *element and its* src *attribute to this method. Also, you use the Google-provided* GSize *constructor to allocate a rectangular section on the map to the photo.*

Question

You're creating a mashup in your application using the Google Maps API and another API that provides news feeds. When a user clicks a location on the map embedded in the application, related news items should appear in a pop-up window. You've already created a PHP proxy to send queries to the second API.

How can you ensure that the news feeds sent by the second API in response are displayed correctly?

Options:

1. Configure a GClientGeocoder instance to extract the news feeds from the response
2. Configure the setCenter() method to specify the location of each pop-up window
3. Parse XML content returned by the second API using the GXml namespace
4. Use the openInfoWindowHtml() method to ensure that news items can appear next to a selected location

Answer

Option 1: This option is incorrect. You use a GClientGeocoder *instance to extract geographical coordinates from Google servers.*

Option 2: This option is incorrect. You use the setCenter() *method to center a Google Maps instance on a specified location.*

Option 3: This option is correct. To create the mashup, you need to transfer content from the second API to your application. You can parse this content using the parse() *method of the* GXml *namespace.*

Option 4: This option is correct. The openInfoWindowHtml() *method enables you to display content extracted from an API over a Google Maps marker.*

Correct answer(s):

3. Parse XML content returned by the second API using the GXml namespace
4. Use the openInfoWindowHtml() method to ensure that news items can appear next to a selected location

Summary

You can use APIs to add fully functional sections of web sites, such as Twitter or Google, to your Ajax applications. Most APIs are freely available and share similarities with web services in the manner in which they present content.

However, unlike web services, APIs don't use any prespecified techniques for data exchange. Instead, each web site offering an API can specify its own data-exchange methods. Also, before you can use an API, you need to create an account at the parent web site and obtain an access key.

Aside from APIs, you can also add mashups to your applications. These mashups combine the functions of two or more APIs or web services to offer a completely new service. To create a mashup, you first call an API or web service in your application. Then you use this API or web service to extract and display content from the other APIs or web services.

Using Web Services and Mashups in Ajax

Learning Objectives

After completing this topic, you should be able to

- *call a web service from an Ajax application*
- *use APIs to create a mashup*

Exercise overview

In this exercise, you're required to call web services from Ajax applications. You're also required to use APIs to create a mashup.

This involves the following tasks:

- calling a web service from an Ajax application via a proxy
- calling a web service from an Ajax application by using the <script> tag hack, and
- using APIs to create a mashup in an Ajax application

Using a proxy to call a web service

You're updating the Ajax web site for WeekendBreak Airways, a company that organizes tours to four US cities. You want to add new features to the web site.

One of these features is the ability to check the current weather in the four cities. To add this feature, you decide to use the Global Weather web service, which is offered by webserviceX.NET.

Because the Global Weather web service is hosted on a separate domain, you decide to call the service from your web site via a proxy, weatherproxy.php. You've already configured this code in the proxy.

Code

```php
<?php
header('Content-Type: text/xml');

$URL
$city = urlencode($_REQUEST['city']);
$URL .= $city;
$xml
echo $xml->saveXML();
?>
```

You've also created an HTML file, weather.html. This file currently contains this code.

Code

```html
<html xmlns="http://www.w3.org/1999/xhtml">
  <head>
    <title>Weather for US cities</title>
  </head>
  <body>
    <form id="weather" name="weather">
    <p>Find the weather at any of our Locations</p>
    <input type="button" onclick="getWeather('Austin');"
      value="Northglenn" />
    <input type="button" onclick="getWeather('Phoenix');"
      value="Phoenix" />
    <input type="button" onclick="getWeather('Los Angeles');"
      value="Los Angeles" />
    <input type="button" onclick="getWeather('Miami');"
      value="Miami" />
    <br /><br />
    <table id="weatherOutput"></table>
    </form>
  </body>
</html>
```

Question

The four buttons you've added to weather.html should allow users to check the weather at the four cities. When a user clicks a button, you want the associated getWeather() function to extract weather details from the web service. You want to specify the code for this function in a JavaScript file named weather.js.

What should you do to complete the coding for the PHP and HTML files?

Options:

1. Call the PHP file in the HTML file via the src attribute of the <body> tag
2. Call the weather.js file in the HTML file via the src attribute of the <script> tag
3. Add the web service endpoint to the PHP file via the url variable
4. Configure the load method to pass on the value stored in url to an XmlDocument instance

Answer

Option 1: This option is incorrect. You don't use the <body> tag to call the PHP file in the JavaScript code. In this tag, you only configure the content that should appear on a web page.

Option 2: This option is correct. The weather.js file contains the getWeather() function. Because you want the buttons in the HTML file to launch this function, you should ensure that the file contains a reference to weather.js.

Option 3: This option is correct. Using the web service endpoint, you send a query to the web service. You should assign this query to the url variable in the PHP file.

Option 4: This option is incorrect. In a PHP file, you use the load *method to pass on a stored query to the* DOMDocument *object. An* XmlDocument *instance belongs to the ASP.NET code.*

Correct answer(s):

2. Call the weather.js file in the HTML file via the src attribute of the <script> tag
3. Add the web service endpoint to the PHP file via the url variable

Question

You're now configuring the getWeather() function in the weather.js file. You want this function to download a response from the web service and then process the response using another function, showWeather().

To ensure that a response can be downloaded, configure the statement that queries the proxy. The query should be about the weather in the city specified by the city variable.

Code

```
var ajax = null;
if (window.XMLHttpRequest)
{
  ajax = new XMLHttpRequest();
} else if (window.ActiveXObject)
{
  ajax = new ActiveXObject("Microsoft.XMLHTTP");
}

function getWeather(city)
{
  ajax.abort();
  var url = "INSERT THE MISSING CODE" + city;
  ajax.open("GET", url, true);
  ajax.onreadystatechange = showWeather;
  ajax.send(null);
}
```

Answer

To ensure that the weather in the specified city is retrieved, you should construct a statement that includes the name of the proxy and the city *attribute.*

Correct answer(s):

1. weatherproxy.php?city=

Question

You've configured the showWeather() function to store the web service response in the XML variable, xmlDoc. You now want to ensure that the XML data in the response is correctly parsed for all types of browsers.

To begin with, you want to configure parsing for Internet Explorer browsers.

What code should you use to do this?

Code

```
function showWeather()
{
 if (ajax.readyState == 4)
 {
  // additional code
  var xmlDoc = null;
  var xmlObject = null;

  if (window.ActiveXObject)
  {
   xmlDoc = XML.childNodes[1].firstChild.nodeValue;
   xmlobject = new ActiveXObject("Microsoft.XMLDOM")
   xmlObject.async="false";
   xmlObject.INSERT THE MISSING CODE;
  }
 }
}
```

Options:

1. loadXML(xmlDoc)
2. responseXML
3. DOMParser

Answer

Option 1: This option is correct. You use the loadXML() *method to send values parsed for Internet Explorer browsers to an* ActiveXObject *instance. You can use this method only after you've extracted XML data from the web-service response and stored the data in a document variable.*

Option 2: This option is incorrect. The responseXML *property stores the web service response. You should've already passed on this property to the* XML *variable.*

Option 3: This option is incorrect. You use the DOMParser *object to parse XML data for Mozilla-based browsers. The* parseFromString() *method of this object enables you to parse the data.*

Correct answer(s):

1. loadXML(xmlDoc)

Using a tag hack to call a web service

Suppose you're creating an Ajax application for an investment firm. In the application, you want to integrate a web service, Zoflina Stock Quotes, which provides hourly stock quotes. This web service sends data only in JSON format. So you decide to use the <script> tag hack to call the service from the Ajax application.

Question

You're configuring the HTML file for the application. You've added a text box and a button to the file. Users can type a company name in the text box and then click the button to receive stock quotes for the company.

165

To handle the click event, you want to use a function named script_hack(). You intend to declare this function in the JavaScript file, quotes.js.

What code should you use to ensure that the click event is handled correctly?

Code
```
<html xmlns="http://www.w3.org/1999/xhtml">
 <head>
  <title>Latest Stock Quotes</title>
  <script type="text/javascript" INSERT THE MISSING CODE></script>
 </head>
 <body>
  <form id="quotes" name="quotes">
  Enter a company name: <input type="text" name="query"
    id="query" />
  <input type="button" onclick="script_hack();"
    value="Get Quotes" />
  <br /><br />
  <table id="output"></table>
  </form>
 </body>
</html>
```

Answer

To be handled correctly, the click *event must have access to the* script_hack() *function. You ensure this by passing on the name of the file that contains this function to the* <script> *tag.*

Correct answer(s):

1. src="quotes.js"

Question

You're now configuring the script_hack() function. In this function, you want to use a JavaScript version of the <script> tag to call the web service. To access the <script> tag in the function, you first want to extract the head element from the HTML file.

What code should you use to do this?

Code
```
function getOutput(JSON)
{
 alert(JSON.ResultSet.totalResultsAvailable+"
   results were found for your search");
}

function script_hack()
{
 var url = "http://search.zoflinaapis.com/StockQuoteService/
   V1/quoteSearch?appid=ZoflinaDem&callback=getOutput
   &output=json&query="+document.search.query.value;
```

```
var head = document.INSERT THE MISSING CODE("head").item(0);
var script = document.createElement("script");
script.setAttribute("type", "text/javascript");
script.setAttribute("src", url);
}
```

Options:

1. getElementsByTagName
2. firstChild.nodeValue
3. createTextNode

Answer

Option 1: This option is correct. The getElementsByTagName() *method allows you to extract the* head *element from the HTML file.*

Option 2: This option is incorrect. You use firstChild.nodeValue *to extract the value stored in the first child element in a Document Object Model structure.*

Option 3: This option is incorrect. You use the createTextNode() *method to extract text from a tag.*

Correct answer(s):

1. getElementsByTagName

Question

In the script_hack() function, you now want to ensure that the src attribute of the script variable can call the web service.

What code should you use to do this?

Code
```
function getOutput(JSON)
{
 alert(JSON.ResultSet.totalResultsAvailable+"
   results were found for your search");
}

function script_hack()
{
 var url = "http://search.zoflinaapis.com/StockQuoteService/
   V1/quoteSearch?appid=ZoflinaDem&callback=getOutput
   &output=json&query="+document.search.query.value;
 // additional code
 var script = document.createElement("script");
 script.setAttribute("type", "text/javascript");
 script.setAttribute("src", url);
 INSERT THE MISSING CODE(script);
}
```

Answer

To ensure that the web service is called, you need to add the script *variable to the* head *element. You use the* appendChild() *method for this.*

Correct answer(s):

1. head.appendChild

Creating a mashup

Case Study: Question 1 of 4

Scenario

For your convenience, the case study is repeated with each question.

You're creating an Ajax web site for Portage Airlines, a flight-charter service. The company has four branch offices in the United States.

On the home page of the web site, you want to embed a portion of Google Maps so that users can easily locate the branch offices. To enable the users to identify each branch office, you want to display its photo when they click the office location on the map.

To quickly implement the requirements, you decide to create a mashup using the Google Maps and Flickr APIs. You start by saving the geographical coordinates of each branch office in the coordinates.xml file. You also create a proxy, flickr.php, to send photo requests to Flickr.

Refer to the learning aid **Current Code Status – Portage Airlines** to review the coding you've done until now. Then create the mashup.

To successfully complete the code for the mashup, answer the questions in order.

Question

You've obtained access keys for the Google and Flickr APIs. You're now configuring the HTML file, home.html, for the home page.

What code should you use to ensure that the home page can call the Google Maps API?

Code
```
<html xmlns="http://www.w3.org/1999/xhtml">
  <head>
    <meta http-equiv="content-type" content="text/html";
     charset=utf-8" />
    <title>Portage Airlines' Offices</title>
    <INSERT THE MISSING CODE"http://maps.google.com/maps?file=api&v=2
     &key=ABQIAAAAZUgQcERqJbKFRuoDh0HM7RT1gBj71UlO4u1BPAtlju0e
     WgO2gBS2OLMRSnXcXKNJ_WLBJNvqZBVlhQ"
     type="text/javascript"></script>
    <script type="text/javascript" src="map.js"></script>
```

```
  </head>
  <body onload="load();">
  <div id="map" style="width: 500px; height: 300px;"></div>
  </body>
</html>
```

Answer

To call the Google Maps API, the home page should recognize the URL of the API. So you pass on this URL to the home page via the src *attribute of the* <script> *tag.*

Correct answer(s):

1. script src=

Case Study: Question 2 of 4

Scenario

For your convenience, the case study is repeated with each question.

You're creating an Ajax web site for Portage Airlines, a flight-charter service. The company has four branch offices in the United States.

On the home page of the web site, you want to embed a portion of Google Maps so that users can easily locate the branch offices. To enable the users to identify each branch office, you want to display its photo when they click the office location on the map.

To quickly implement the requirements, you decide to create a mashup using the Google Maps and Flickr APIs. You start by saving the geographical coordinates of each branch office in the coordinates.xml file. You also create a proxy, flickr.php, to send photo requests to Flickr.

Refer to the learning aid **Current Code Status – Portage Airlines** to review the coding you've done until now. Then create the mashup.

To successfully complete the code for the mashup, answer the questions in order.

Question

You're now configuring the JavaScript file for the home page.

What code should you use to ensure that the file can retrieve photos from Flickr?

Code
```
var map = null;
var geocoder = null;
var imageUrl = '';

function load(e)
{
 if (GBrowserIsCompatible())
 {
```

```
  map = new GMap2(document.getElementById("map"));
  geocoder = new GClientGeocoder();
  addMarkers();
 }
}

function getImageURL(address)
{
 INSERT THE MISSING CODE("flickr.php?api=flickr.photos.search
   &key=8884e9cf45ddd9899f554cb0a423f7d6&param_key=text
   &param_value="+address, function(data, responseCode) {
 var xml = GXml.parse(data);
 var photos = xml.documentElement.getElementsByTagName("photo");
 var server = photos[0].getAttribute("server");
 var id = photos[0].getAttribute("id");
 var secret = photos[0].getAttribute("secret");
})
}
```

Options:

1. GDownloadUrl
2. GXmlHttp
3. load($url)

Answer

Option 1: *This option is correct. The* GDownloadUrl *function enables you to asynchronously retrieve content by using the proxy file. In the query that you create for the proxy, you attach the API key and the variable that stores the branch office addresses.*

Option 2: *This option is incorrect. You can't use the* GXmlHttp *namespace directly. You first need to declare its instance. Also, when using* GXmlHttp, *you need to add code to verify the value of the* readyState *property.*

Option 3: *This option is incorrect. You use the* load($URL) *command in a PHP file. This command passes on a query statement stored in the* URL *variable to the* DOMDocument *object.*

Correct answer(s):

1. GDownloadUrl

Case Study: Question 3 of 4

Scenario

For your convenience, the case study is repeated with each question.

You're creating an Ajax web site for Portage Airlines, a flight-charter service. The company has four branch offices in the United States.

On the home page of the web site, you want to embed a portion of Google Maps so that users can easily locate the branch offices. To enable the users to identify each branch office, you want to display its photo when they click the office location on the map.

To quickly implement the requirements, you decide to create a mashup using the Google Maps and Flickr APIs. You start by saving the geographical coordinates of each branch office in the coordinates.xml file. You also create a proxy, flickr.php, to send photo requests to Flickr.

Refer to the learning aid **Current Code Status – Portage Airlines** to review the coding you've done until now. Then create the mashup.

To successfully complete the code for the mashup, answer the questions in order.

Question

Now configure the imageUrl variable to store the source URLs of the photos you want to download. When doing so, ensure that each downloaded photo measures 240 pixels on the longest side.

Code

```
function load(e)
{
  if (GBrowserIsCompatible())
  {
    map = new GMap2(document.getElementById("map"));
    geocoder = new GClientGeocoder();
    addMarkers();
  }
}

function getImageURL(address)
{
  //additional code
  {
    var xml = GXml.parse(data);
    var photos = xml.documentElement.getElementsByTagName("photo");
    var server = photos[0].getAttribute("server");
    var id = photos[0].getAttribute("id");
    var secret = photos[0].getAttribute("secret");
    imageUrl = "http://static.flickr.com/"+server+"/"+id
      +"_"INSERT THE MISSING CODE.jpg";
    alert (imageUrl);
  })
}
```

Answer

A source URL for a photo should contain the ID of the server that stores the photo. The URL should also specify the ID, secret key, and dimensions for the photo. So you complete the coding for the given URL by adding the secret variable, which stores the secret key, and the letter m, *which specifies the required dimensions.*

Correct answer(s):

1. +secret+"_m

Case Study: Question 4 of 4

For your convenience, the case study is repeated with each question.

You're creating an Ajax web site for Portage Airlines, a flight-charter service. The company has four branch offices in the United States.

On the home page of the web site, you want to embed a portion of Google Maps so that users can easily locate the branch offices. To enable the users to identify each branch office, you want to display its photo when they click the office location on the map.

To quickly implement the requirements, you decide to create a mashup using the Google Maps and Flickr APIs. You start by saving the geographical coordinates of each branch office in the coordinates.xml file. You also create a proxy, flickr.php, to send photo requests to Flickr.

Refer to the learning aid **Current Code Status – Portage Airlines** to review the coding you've done until now. Then create the mashup.

To successfully complete the code for the mashup, answer the questions in order.

Question

In the JavaScript file, you're now configuring a function that adds markers at the office locations.

Ensure that the openInfoWindowHtml() method can allocate space for the photo associated with any location a user clicks.

Code

```
}

function addMarkers(address, e)
{
 GDownloadUrl("coordinates.xml", function(data, responseCode) {
 var xml = GXml.parse(data);
 var markers = xml.documentElement.getElementsByTagName("location");
 for (var i=0; i<markers.length; i++)
  {
   point2 = new GLatLng(parseFloat(markers[i].getAttribute("lat")),
    parseFloat(markers[i].getAttribute("lng")));
   map.setCenter(point2, 13);
   map.setZoom(3);
   marker2 = new GMarker(point2);
   map.addOverlay(marker2);
   var imageUrl = getImageURL(markers[i].getAttribute("address"));
   alert(imageUrl);
   GEvent.addListener(marker2,"click",
    (function (marker, pImageurl) {
     return function() { marker.openInfoWindowHtml
     ("<img src='"+pImageurl+"' />", INSERT THE MISSING CODE(200,200)); }
    })(marker2, imageUrl));
  }
})
}
```

Answer

To ensure that the openInfoWindowHtml() *method can allocate space for a photo, you set the* GSize *constructor. This Google-provided constructor creates a rectangular section over the map to accommodate a photo.*

Correct answer(s):

1. new GSize

Web services have been called in Ajax applications via a proxy and by using the <script> tag hack. Additionally, two APIs have been used to create a mashup in an Ajax application.

www.ingramcontent.com/pod-product-compliance
Lightning Source LLC
Chambersburg PA
CBHW080554060326

40689CB00021B/4856